Troublesome Children in Class

Troublesome Children in Class

Irene E. Caspari

Department for Children and Parents,
Tavistock Clinic, London

ROUTLEDGE & KEGAN PAUL
LONDON AND BOSTON

First published in 1976
by Routledge & Kegan Paul Ltd
Broadway House, 68-74 Carter Lane,
London EC4V 5EL and
9 Park Street,
Boston, Mass. 02108, USA
Set in ten point Pilgrim on eleven and half point body
and printed in Great Britain by
Northumberland Press Ltd, Gateshead
© Irene E. Caspari 1976

ISBN 0 7100 8261 4 (c)
      0 7100 8262 2 (p)

The Students Library of Education has been designed to meet the needs of students of Education at Colleges of Education and at University Institutes and Departments. It will also be valuable for practising teachers and educationists. The series takes full account of the latest developments in teacher-training and of new methods and approaches in education. Separate volumes will provide authoritative and up-to-date accounts of the topics within the major fields of sociology, philosophy and history of education, educational psychology, and method. Care has been taken that specialist topics are treated lucidly and usefully for the non-specialist reader. Altogether, the Students Library of Education will provide a comprehensive introduction and guide to anyone concerned with the study of educational theory and practice.

To Billy Tibble

who asked me to write this book
and who sadly is no longer here to see it

Contents

Acknowledgments

It would be difficult to count the many people who have made this book possible. There are the large number of children I have taught at school, many of whom appear in this book. There are the teachers, who helped with some of the research studies and those that shared with me their ideas and their concern about education; and there are the troublesome children themselves, who form the focus of this book. My thanks go to all these. The children's names are of course disguised.

I am also much indebted for the help and support given by my colleagues at the Tavistock Clinic, particularly by Yana Popper, who has never ceased to take an interest in my pursuits which form the basis of this book. I am equally grateful to the students in educational psychology and those of other training groups for stimulating my thinking.

I should also like to express my gratitude to Elizabeth Irvine, Beryl Sandford and John Bowlby for helping me, each in his or her special way, to further my skills in the art of writing.

My very special thanks go to Marjorie Hourd and Ben Morris for reading this manuscript and for the many helpful suggestions they made.

Finally, I should like to give grateful thanks to Margaret

ACKNOWLEDGMENTS

Walker for her library assistance and to Angela Buesnel, who so efficiently deciphered my hieroglyphics and so cheerfully coped with the typing of the manuscript.

Introduction

This book is about children who appear to be unhappy and disgruntled, who disrupt our classes, who do not seem to derive as much benefit from our teaching as we would hope; children who interrupt a lesson by shouting or fighting each other, children who do not learn, children who destroy another child's work.

These children are to be found in all classes. Some will only be naughty at times, and will settle down again sooner or later when the particular problem is resolved. They will respond to praise, encouragement and kindness, whilst expression of displeasure will generally check undesirable behaviour. Only occasionally is more severe punishment necessary. Others, however, seem to be more frequently naughty, they react neither to a heart-to-heart talk nor to punishment, they say that they are sorry but none the less continue as before. It is extraordinarily difficult to distinguish clearly between these two kinds of behaviour. There are no definite characteristics that belong to one group and are absent in the other. Only if the whole behaviour pattern is taken into account does the difference between the ordinary naughty child and the child with severe emotional difficulties become apparent.

In this book I shall attempt, among other things, to throw some light on the most outstanding patterns of behaviour that distinguish the one type of children from the other. Naturally these will be linked to home conditions, such as the socio-economic set-up or the child's relationship to his parents and siblings. To look for possible causes of a child's behaviour patterns in these regions is a commonplace nowadays. It is, however, also common experience that it is often very difficult to gain accurate information about these factors, particularly about those connected with home conditions. Nobody wants to wash the family's dirty linen in public. It cannot be expected that a mother would tell a headteacher about her husband's criminal pursuits, although these may cause great anxiety both in her and in her child and might, indeed, be one of the main reasons for the child's deviant behaviour in school. Equally and in a much less dramatic way, a mother who much prefers another sibling to the child in question, might do her best to hide this fact from anyone at school for fear of being criticised by the teachers. There are hundreds of situations where information of this kind might be withheld and distorted, and often for very understandable reasons.

Moreover, this kind of information, even if it is reliable, is only of limited use in the day-to-day relationship between the teacher and the children in the classroom. It will, of course, increase his understanding of the child's behaviour and will influence his reaction towards the child, in as far as he will know that the objectionable behaviour is not entirely directed towards him. But he can rarely discuss these aspects of the child's anxieties with him unless the information has been provided by the child. For this reason I shall also examine other aspects of the external situation such as the stresses to which all children are exposed in the classroom and in the school as a whole. These stresses may even be beneficial in themselves but may ask for a greater ability to adjust than some children can achieve. For example, refusal to learn can sometimes be understood in these terms.

In addition, I shall try to elucidate some of the factors that make up the 'teacher-pupil relationship'. People often talk so glibly about this that the term is in danger of becoming meaningless jargon. In connection with this I shall, of course, look at the children's feelings in an attempt to understand their behaviour. But I shall also look at the teacher's feelings in his dealings with his class and with the troublesome children within it. Much stress will be laid on the importance of understanding the children's feelings and our own in relationship to them as a key towards reducing the frequency and severity of their troublesome behaviour.

However, we all know that we cannot ever entirely understand the feelings of another human being. So too, we should not expect to gain perfect understanding of ourselves, particularly if we include the many levels of understanding ranging from intellectual conceptualisation, which can be discussed and disputed, to intuitive understanding for which there is often no rational explanation. Even if we had this perfect understanding could we really expect to be able to lay down rules and regulations that would enable us to eliminate troublesome behaviour in the children we teach? Some teachers, we know, can reduce these to a minimum, and with perfect understanding methods might, indeed, be developed that might profit all. As things are this is surely not possible. Consequently, we will not describe techniques of acquiring control in the classroom. Yet, I believe that even with imperfect understanding the *wish* to understand our children and ourselves in relationship to them has a profound effect on this relationship and on our ability to deal with troublesome children. Based on this kind of understanding each teacher will need to work out his own way of doing it, and in doing so will, I think, help these troublesome children far more than rules and regulations could ever do, even if they could be devised.

This book is seen as an attempt to explain why this should be so.

Part One

Ordinary children in the classroom

1
Troublesome behaviour of ordinary children and how it is affected by the classroom situation

Many of us are inclined to resent the naughty behaviour of the children we teach, particularly if we care for them and wish to further their development in every possible way.

Yet why should children *not* be troublesome? If we are honest with ourselves is there any person who is not troublesome at times? Is there any successful marriage without any disagreement between the partners? Is there any mother who does not wish her beloved child miles away when she is tired or exhausted or preoccupied with household chores? Is it not known that a quarrel will often strengthen the bond between lovers rather than weaken it? Yet do we not all feel desperately guilty and unhappy afterwards, and do we not even try to hide any inkling of such feelings from other people and indeed often refuse to admit them even to ourselves?

The significance of ambivalent feelings

In 1910 Bleuler described the phenomenon of contradictory feelings towards people who are close to us and Freud (1909, 1926) developed this concept of ambivalent feelings as it was revealed by his patients. As time went on it became more and more apparent that this conflict is part of human life. In an article called 'Psycho-analysis and child care' (1958), Bowlby points out that 'the healthy are divided from the sick' principally by their ability to come to terms with such conflicts. He extends these ideas to child rearing and develops them particularly in respect of the ways in which parents can provide opportunities for healthy development. 'Nothing helps a child more,' he says, 'than being able to express his hostile and jealous feelings candidly, directly and spontaneously and there is no parental task more valuable, I believe, than being able to accept with equanimity such expressions of filial piety as "I hate you, mummy" or "daddy, you are a beast".' Bowlby also suggests that it helps if parents can find ways of expressing their hostile feelings towards their children, when they occur, but in both cases the intensity of these feelings must be within the limits that the other can bear.

Teachers are, of course, also concerned with the up-bringing of children, and these contradictory feelings enter therefore unavoidably into the relationship between the teacher and his class. Yet in practice, teachers tend not to make allowances for the expressions of hostile feelings towards them, although they know that they will come to the surface somehow. For instance, every teacher accepts that a new class will 'try him out' after a short 'honeymoon period'. Most teachers accept this as a necessary evil inherent in their work. They would avoid it if they could. They certainly do not think that this particular situation is of value to the children they teach.

Of course, parents do not particularly relish the expression of negative feelings either. It is, however, becoming more and more accepted that feelings of dislike can be safely expressed at home. Parents usually know that they are also liked and are not too bothered about it. Many teachers, however, become very worried at the expression of negative feelings towards them.

For instance, many teachers experience that the 'being tried out' in a new class is mainly done by just one 'rebel' or a small group of them. An experienced teacher knows that his future relationship with the class will depend on the 'successful' solution to the problem that the challenge of the 'rebels' poses, and that this in turn depends on his ability to find a solution which will control the rebels' feelings without rejecting them. Often teachers link this phenomenon to the specific difficulties of these 'rebels', and it is generally true that such children have a number of problems. However, teachers will also notice the interest and the fascination with which the whole class watches the developments of this challenge.

Group dynamics and behaviour patterns in the classroom

In my opinion this is largely connected with the fact that these 'rebels' are also expressing the feelings of the other members of the class. In this way they can experience the feelings, but need not bear the consequences of their actions, i.e. they need not feel guilty about their behaviour. Observations of behaviour patterns in small adult groups demonstrate how frequently this phenomenon occurs (Bion, 1961).

Small groups have been studied over many years. Morris (1965) gives a very full account of the different kinds of small groups and their relevance to education. Herbert (1961) and Richardson (1951) describe their own experience with small groups in this field. Their work is mainly based on Bion's hypothesis. Richardson (1967) extends these ideas directly to school classes.

The interrelationship within classes at school is, of course, not identical to that within a small group in which group members can easily interact with each other. There are too many pupils in each class to make this intimate face-to-face relationship possible. However, on account of the familiarity of the members of the group a school class cannot be classified as a large group either. Yet some of the phenomena that are observable in large groups seem to contribute greatly to the understanding of the interrelationships in a school class.

Apart from Freud's (1921) original work, psycho-analytically orientated studies of large groups as contrasted to small groups are fairly recent. For instance, Turquet, in an unpublished paper (1973), points to the very special conflict of each member of a large group between retaining his own identity and merging his identity with that of the large group.

My own experience as a member of a conference on Intragroup and Intergroup Relationships, organised jointly by Leicester University and the Tavistock Institute of Human Relations, highlighted many other differences between the group dynamics of small and large groups.

Of the large group experience three aspects seemed to me particularly relevant to school classes:

1 The members of a large group are far more dependent on the leader than they are in a small group. This means that all feelings, positive and negative, are primarily concentrated on the leader, and that these feelings also include those that the group members have for each other. This would mean that the hostile feelings expressed by the 'rebels' towards the teacher include also those that they have towards the other members of the class.

2 To make an impact on the leader and on the other members of the group an individual member has to express his feelings very forcefully, or the same feelings have to be expressed by a large number of group members. In fact, during the rebellion phase in school the single rebel is usually a very forceful person, or the group of rebels is large enough to make an impact. Otherwise the feelings are ignored by the rest of the class.

3 It seems much easier to express destructive feelings in a large group than positive ones, in contrast to a small group where both kinds of feelings are constantly expressed and where there is much more opportunity for reconciliation.

These observations seem of particular concern to education, because learning can only take place in a favourable

10

environment. As Morris (1965) points out, 'To be favourable, learning experiences ... should provide us with roles which enable us to develop the kinds of relationships in terms of which our ideal self image is cast.' Nobody is likely to accept the image of a hostile, destructive person as an ideal. It follows that in a situation in which feelings that are expressed are generally hostile, always very forceful and generally expressed towards the leader, the teacher will be inclined to avoid the expression of these feelings in order to safeguard a favourable learning situation. In this way the opportunity for expressing ambivalent feelings is limited, and with good reason. This does not mean that the expression of ambivalent feelings in class can never be accepted.

Ambivalent feelings in the classroom

For example, many years ago when I was a form-mistress in a grammar school I had to deal with the problem of 'crushes' with a class of 15-year-old girls. In this class having a 'crush' on the teacher had become a preoccupation, with a result that the academic standard of the class had deteriorated. This deterioration was actually discovered by the headmistress and, with her support, I discussed this matter with the girls and stressed the importance of being able to concentrate on one's work even if one has intensive feelings, be it towards a teacher or towards a boyfriend or husband later on in life. The following term many of the girls had improved considerably and some did better than ever before.

In this case the expression of feelings had not led to behaviour problems, but to deterioration of work, which can, of course, also be seen as an expression of hostile feelings. When a pupil's work deteriorates the teacher is inclined to blame the child for the deterioration, but he also blames himself and feels it to be a rejection although he is not always sure of this. I cannot remember having

11

had any feelings about my own failure in my teaching of those girls, but this might be due to the very skilful support of the headmistress. The important thing was, I think, that I could discuss the matter without reproaching the girls and without blaming myself. I was able to accept both their hostile feelings and their feelings of love by discussing the problem in general terms and by making clear that everybody else, myself included, had to come to terms with this conflict. On the surface the conflict appeared to be about concentration and preoccupation with other feelings, but it can also be seen in terms of liking a teacher and rejecting her. After all these girls loved their teachers; their hostility was expressed via the deterioration of the work they did for them. Of course they were not aware of this, nor was I at the time.

There are many occasions when it is not quite so easy to deal with such situations. The problem for the teacher is really similar to that of the parent. The important criterion is that the intensity of the contradictory feelings must be within the limits of what each individual teacher can bear and that the teacher needs to feel that, in spite of the difficult behaviour, he is liked and accepted. Teachers, of course, vary in their capacity to do this as much as parents do. If the expression of contradictory feelings succeeds in disrupting the activity of a large group then the experience of these feelings can no longer be beneficial. They will be followed by intensive guilt feelings. These in themselves do no harm, in fact they are necessary in all relationships. However, as there is so little opportunity for reconciliation in a large group, these guilt feelings cannot easily be used constructively to make amends. This in turn may have a negative effect on the development of the personality since emotional difficulties usually arise from bottled-up feelings, either consciously or unconsciously. For these reasons it is tremendously important that feelings expressed in a class towards the teacher can be contained and controlled by him. Only in this way can the teacher create the framework within which feelings can be expressed and yet be kept within bounds. Of course, if a teacher suppresses all expression of feelings and will not have any of it, the activity of the class, i.e. the learning, will be adversely affected. On the other hand, permissiveness will only be beneficial within reason. There is no doubt that it is a most difficult task for the teacher to allow the expression of unacceptable feelings such as hostility within a 'safe' framework. It is often impossible to do so if these feelings are directly expressed. However, teachers can help their pupils to express them in more indirect and more acceptable ways, namely through the curriculum itself. This will be discussed later on.

2

The child: stresses in the classroom situation

Stress, like conflict, is something of a 'dirty' word. Being 'under stress' or 'in a conflict situation' is a state to be avoided. In the previous chapter I have already used the term 'conflict' in a slightly different way, viz. as a human condition common to us all with which we have to come to terms. In what follows I shall use 'stress' in a similar way. I see 'a stress situation' as a challenge to the individual demanding a change of behaviour. All un-familiar situations, for instance, are stressful in this sense of the word. At the same time they are interesting and exciting. Our self-esteem and self-confidence depends greatly on our ability to tolerate this kind of stress and to overcome it. Only if stress situations are beyond the limits of endurance, will they be harmful and result in disturbing behaviour. The trouble is that these limits will vary from individual to individual. What might be an exciting challenge for one may be an insolu-able dilemma for another. As the demand for change is an integral part of education, all educational settings cause a certain amount of stress, which in turn may lead to troublesome behaviour. It seems therefore useful to examine in some detail those stresses for the child and the teacher that are inherent in the classroom situation, stresses that are a challenge to some, who adjust and grow through this challenge, but which may equally be too much for others.

Klein (1962) in a chapter on 'Problems in adjustment to school' mentions three areas of stress that challenge the child: the separation of the child from his family, particularly from his mother; the need to adhere to the demands of 'task orientation' as Klein calls it, in other words to focus on the task, i.e. the learning; and lastly, the demand to adjust to a large number of peers with whom the child has to share the attention of one adult, the teacher.

Separation from the mother and the family

The effects of separation on the pre-school child at hospitalisation have been very lucidly demonstrated by Bowlby (1973) and Robertson (1962) and are widely accepted. However, little consideration is given to the possibility that similar, though less intensive, anxieties might exist at school entry. This is not really surprising for it is extraordinarily painful to watch a young child's distress. It is well known that nurses are inclined to deny the signs of unhappiness expressed by children in hospital, so it is not particularly astonishing that teachers and parents are often not fully aware of the child's distress when he first goes to primary school. The impact of this separation is more frequently recognised in nursery schools where the children are younger and mothers are often encouraged to stay with their child for the first few days.

Infant school teachers at reception classes are well aware of this stress, but usually link it to the presence of the parents. They say that the children are restless as long as the parents are there, but that they settle down when the parents have gone. There is, of course, some truth in this observation as children are inclined to protest as long as they feel that there is a chance of avoiding the separation. When they find that they have to accept the situation they are more likely to become withdrawn and quiet, and it is difficult to distinguish this kind of behaviour from the genuine settling down of other children of this age.

Some years ago I received a verbal report from an educational psychologist, who observed a reception class in an infant school during the first day of school. He gave several instances of such stressful behaviour after the parents had left, but just as the nurses in hospital do not notice the withdrawn behaviour of small children in the hustle and bustle of life on a hospital ward, the infant teacher can easily miss similar behaviour in the hurly-burly of an infant class.

The child does, of course, not only feel that his mother has left him, he also leaves his younger siblings at home. This can lead to intense jealousy which can be expressed in various ways; at home it might lead to sleeplessness or minor illnesses that prevent the child from going to school; at school he might appear inattentive and irritable.

Task orientation

The need to comply with the demands of the 'task orientation' at school is also very difficult for the young child. Of course he has to comply now and then with the wishes of his parents and siblings at home, but in school his activities are determined by the wishes of the teacher and the rules of the school most of the time. He has to begin and to finish whatever he is doing when the bell goes, he has to occupy himself with the tasks that the teacher suggests, be it reading, number work, hand-work, or listening to a story or doing PE. He has to line up before he goes to Assembly or to meals. He has to be silent on various occasions, and when he talks he must not talk too loudly so as not to disturb the other children. This demand to attend to activities, concentrate on learning matter and comply with the rules necessary for communal living are very important elements of education at all ages. Of course, the maturity of the pupils is always taken into account, particularly with the very young child, but a certain degree of compulsion is unavoidable. Again there is no harm in this, and indeed it is a very important factor in the preparation for work in adult life. But again, if any individual child is forced too much, troublesome behaviour will ensue. In this case, 'troublesome behaviour' might be expressed by the child's unwillingness to learn, and it is very difficult for the teacher to distinguish this type of behaviour from that of the child who does not progress on account of low intellectual ability.

Relationships with peers

The third area of adjustment problems mentioned by Klein concerns the child's ability to gain acceptance by his peers. Again, so little systematic work has been done in this area that I have to fall back on my own observations with several groups of primary school children. I have found that there are certain rituals connected with gaining an accepted position in a peer group. These vary for the sexes. A boy seems to have to prove himself in a physical fight. He has to show that he can stand up for himself, but he must also demonstrate that he can control his strength so as to avoid excessive damage to his opponent. He is generally put to the test very soon after he joins the group.

Girls, on the other hand, are generally very friendly to each other at first, but I have often observed that a group of girls, who have played happily with each other for days, will suddenly reject one of their mates in a vicious manner and will only accept her again after she has shown that she can deal with this rejection. Generally this takes the form of someone saying, 'I don't want to play with you.' This rejection will be taken up by other members of the group and she will only be accepted as a member of the group again if she can show that she can find another group of girls to play with her.

This problem of peer acceptance makes considerable

demands on a child. For instance, the boy who stands up for a fight must unavoidably be aggressive, but not to the extent of really hurting the other child, and therefore needs a considerable amount of self-control to meet this challenge successfully. The same is true of the girl, who has to be able to care about being expelled by her friends and yet appear as if she does not care. The processes are possibly far more complicated than these simple observations would suggest. What is important in the context of this discussion is that peer relationships provide an area of considerable stress to children of all ages.

The child and the teacher

Lastly, I should like to mention the teacher himself or herself. The teacher is, of course, the most important person in the classroom for all children; he is the only adult in this situation and the child's activities are regulated mainly by him. He is also the leader of the large group, on whom all the group members are so utterly dependent. No wonder that every child is greatly concerned as to whether or not the teacher likes him and appreciates his work, so much so that his interpretation of the teacher's behaviour might be quite unrealistic.

At one time, for instance, I had great difficulties with a group of adolescent girls to whom I taught German. They were often inattentive, they talked a great deal and seemed discontented. After a while I began to realise that they disliked me because I frequently corrected their German pronunciation. To me, this seemed to be part of my job, but they obviously felt that I was critical of them as people and as a result they became troublesome.

There are a number of reasons why pupils may have a slightly distorted view of their teacher's behaviour and attitudes. Some of these can be linked to the way in which we see all other people's behaviour to some extent in terms of our own feelings. This is one of the major assumptions in all psycho-analytically orientated theories of behaviour. The teacher, as the leader of the group, is, of course, more exposed to such distorted interpretations than most people.

The teacher as assessor of the child's work

However, I should like to highlight a much more mundane reason for such misinterpretations of the teacher's behaviour, which is entirely linked to his role as a teacher, particularly, to his duty to assess the child's work and to communicate this assessment both to the child and to the child's parents. Just as the girls in their German class interpreted my attempts to improve their pronunciation as a criticism of themselves, every pupil is likely to feel a 'good' mark as a token of acceptance by the teacher and a 'bad' mark as a rejection. Of course the degree to which this is felt to be so varies from individual to individual. The pupil's view is also likely to become more realistic with increasing maturity. This is generally recognised. In most infant schools, for instance, teachers rarely comment on children's poor work. Mock 'O' level examinations on the other hand are often marked very critically.

The extent to which children's attitudes towards a subject are influenced by the teacher's assessment is illustrated by an enquiry I conducted into the attitude of grammar school girls towards French. Although I did not analyse the results systematically, it became clear that there was a considerable degree of correlation between each pupil's examination results in French and her attitude towards the subject in comparison with other subjects. Those that had obtained a good result liked French better than those that had not, even though some of them showed very clearly on a different questionnaire that they disliked most of the activities that went on during French lessons. This was in spite of the fact that the examination results did not represent the pupils' efficiency in French. Each year was streamed for ability in French and mathematics, so that the examination papers set for the lowest stream were far easier than those set for the more advanced streams. The girls were quite aware of this, but that did not change their attitude. At the time I did not explore to what extent the girls' attitude to the subject also reflected their attitude to the teacher. However, as a preliminary before this enquiry I asked a number of adults whether they liked French at school, and if they gave a positive answer and I asked them why, the general reply was that they liked the teacher. It is, of course, difficult to know which is the chicken and which is the egg. Did they like the teacher because they were successful, or were they successful because they worked hard for the teacher they liked?

The trouble is that the teacher's assessment can be objective only in tasks where there is a definite correct or incorrect response, such as arithmetic or Latin prose. With all 'open-ended' activities, such as essays, the teacher's assessment is unavoidably influenced by his own preferences. Often one hears pupils say; 'I just cannot write essays for Miss X or for Mr Y.' Sometimes this might be a justification for the pupil's own inadequacies, but frequently it is a fairly realistic assessment of the situation. Unavoidably, teachers assess the child's work in terms of their own expectations. In a teachers' discussion group, for instance, a very sensitive and capable teacher in a junior school mentioned the poor quality of a boy's essays. She found them odd and wondered how she could help the boy. She gave us an example. The theme of the essay had been 'A Winter's Night' and she expected a description of a cold crisp night in winter, or a stormy night or perhaps an account of an adventure on such a night. The boy described himself in a cosy, warm room, looking out onto the snow-covered landscape when he heard a fierce knock on the door. He opened the door and outside was a vicious monster. The story was well told for a boy of 8 or 9. When we discussed the essay and suggested that the story might be looked at in terms of a dream, the teacher could suddenly appreciate its literary value. She had also been worried about some of the disturbing aspects of the story, such as the very frightening description of the monster. As an outsider one could understand and sympathise with the teacher's reaction. One wonders what the boy had felt about it. From the teacher's description of his behaviour in school it was clear that he was a boy with many problems. The teacher was aware of this and anxious to help him, but had been unable to understand his communication.

This example illustrates, I hope, how easily a teacher's assessment might be influenced by his or her own preoccupations, and to what extent the teacher's judgment influences the relationship between himself and his pupils.

However, the child does not only experience the teacher as the assessor of his work. The teacher is also the only adult in the classroom and troublesome behaviour can easily arise because of the need for each child to share this one caring adult with so many other children. Again it is important for each child's future life to come to terms with this situation, but if a child has intensive needs for encouragement by an adult he will show his resentment by what is generally called 'attention-seeking' behaviour. This takes numerous forms. Sometimes a child gains the teacher's attention by quarrelling with another child, sometimes he calls out, sometimes he comes up to the teacher to ask whether he can be of help when the teacher is preoccupied with something else. This kind of behaviour can be extremely irritating, particularly when the child in question cannot gain the teacher's attention by good work.

Stresses of adjustment at different age levels

Stresses of adjustment in school vary, of course, with the age of the child. Stresses caused through the need to leave the family, for instance, will be felt generally by the very young child but will very rarely be a problem for an adolescent. Similarly, the adolescent will experience adjustment problems of considerable dimensions that have not appeared before the pupil enters this period of development.

Adolescents are often very preoccupied with their feelings and their behaviour is very often erratic. At one time they want to be looked after like very young children, at other times they oppose whatever those in authority say. This in itself is part of natural development, a way of freeing oneself from the dependence on adults and of gaining the autonomy necessary for adult life. Naturally, adults find this fluctuation between dependence and rebellion very difficult to tolerate. The teacher who is able to accept this behaviour can therefore make a tremendous contribution towards the development of young people. Nobody, however, should be under the illusion that this is an easy task.

These are, of course, only a few of the stresses that the classroom situation exerts on the children we teach. Every one of these children experiences this situation in his own individual way, according to his own individual experiences in the past. All institutions demand adaptation from the individual. Schools are no exception. Yet, if we want to help those of our children who worry us by their troublesome behaviour, it seems advisable to examine to what extent the school situation in general and the classroom situation in particular may contribute towards that behaviour. The understanding alone will be helpful. A change in the situation may often be advisable. Sometimes it is the most effective way of helping the child.

3

Stresses on the teacher at school

When we looked at the stresses to which the pupils are exposed we concentrated mainly on the classroom situation as the setting in which most children spend most of their time in most schools. With the arrival of team-teaching, teaching aids such as teaching-machines and television and with an increasingly complicated tutorial system in secondary schools, the situation is likely to shift. At present, however, most children are still taught in classroom situations.

Teachers also spend a large part of their working life in classrooms. Yet the teacher's stresses in the classroom cannot be understood unless other aspects of the teacher's professional life are taken into account. In this chapter I propose to examine the pressures on the teacher in the classroom, as well as in relationship to other aspects of his life in school.

The teacher's role

The teacher's role has been scrutinised by many writers. Morris (1972) for instance points to stresses on the teacher arising from poor pay and from being exclusively in contact with immature minds. Hoyle (1969) refers to the teacher's growing insecurity arising from modern society's uncertainty about basic values, while Wilson (1962) discusses the lack of a clear job definition which makes a teacher's position extremely difficult.

It can, for instance, be argued that apart from examination results, there are no tangible criteria on which a teacher's work can be judged. If a child is happy at school, if he is successful in his work, interested in his lessons and enjoying many out-of-school activities, by what criteria can this be linked to the excellence of the teaching? To what extent might the success be due to the child's personality or to the influences at home? Alternatively, if the child fails at school, if he does not get on with his teachers and his peers, if he prefers to stay at home, to what extent is the teacher to blame, to what extent is the failure due to lack of ability or immaturity of the child, or problems at home? In general, 'good' schools seem to have more successful pupils. However, they also attract more children from more adequate homes, and the evidence from systematic studies (Douglas, 1964 and Pringle, 1974) suggests that children's success or failure at school are very closely linked to parental attitudes and that children can be severely handicapped at school by lack of educational opportunities in the home during the early years of a child's life. This insecurity inevitably increases any stresses that a teacher experiences in his work. Most important of all, it leads to a reluctance to share his problems with other people, because the teacher himself finds it difficult to judge to what extent these problems may be due to his own inefficiency. It is not at all easy to find the right balance between blaming oneself for everything that goes wrong and assuming that the fault can always be found in the child or in the home.

There are, in my opinion, three main areas of immediate concern for a teacher in the classroom : the knowledge of the subject matter; the methods and ways of presenting the subject matter to the children he teaches; and how to keep discipline in class.

The teacher's concern about his knowledge of the subject matter

In my experience the knowledge of the subject is of most concern to young and relatively inexperienced teachers, who fear to lose face if they do not know every detail of the subject matter. It stands to reason, of course, that a teacher needs to know what he wants to teach, but this is often understood in terms of his having all the details at his fingertips. In my opinion this is hardly ever necessary. A primary school teacher, for instance, or a teacher taking general subjects in secondary schools can always read up what he needs to know and consult his notes if need be, like any lecturer in a university. Teachers of special skills, such as a foreign language, or those that prepare their pupils for advanced examinations can only do so after some years of study and usually know far more about their subject than their pupils ever need to learn. Of course, teachers can make mistakes. They may be asked a question to which they do not know the answer. Some teachers feel that they may lose the children's respect if they confess their ignorance, yet I have never found this to be so. On the contrary, it seemed to be a very valuable experience for the pupils. If I, the teacher, could admit to my lack of knowledge without feeling ashamed of it, the children found it easier to bear their own ignorance. Frequently I encouraged them to find the answer so that they could instruct me. This kind of role reversal can have a very beneficial effect on the rate of children's learning, if used sensibly and sparingly.

Of course, lessons need to be prepared. The primary school teacher introducing his pupils to the mechanics of the steam engine has to devote some time to studying this subject even if sufficient information can be gained from consulting the *Children's Encyclopaedia*. The French teacher reading Molière's *Tartuffe* with some sixth form students will have to re-read the play and consult his notes. Moreover, all teachers need to give some thought to the amount of information they wish to present and how it might be presented.

The teacher's concern about methods and ways of presentation

This is, in my opinion, a much more complicated task. Much will depend on the subject matter, on the age of the children, on their maturity level, on their ability, on the size of the class, even on the size and shape of the classroom. Certain ways of presentation that worked well one day might be a complete flop on the next occasion. A particular approach might work with one particular group but not with another. On the one hand the teacher needs to make a plan, on the other hand, he might have to change it on the spur of the moment.

The skill involved in the organisation of the lesson and the presentation of the material is often underrated. Even the most ordinary activity, such as a reading or arithmetic lesson to 7–8-year-olds is a most complicated task.

At this age the pupils will be on different levels of efficiency in these subjects. Therefore few teachers would decide on a class lesson, although some might, and at times it might be the most appropriate way of approach. However, if there is a more individual approach, the teacher has a number of choices: he can divide the class into groups, he can ask them to work individually or in pairs. He has to decide what apparatus to use and how to check up on what each child actually has learned and he has to judge how long to continue with each activity and so on. If the teacher wishes to familiarise his pupils with facts, he needs to consider the age level and maturity level of his group, as well as the particular idiosyncrasies of the particular group of children he teaches. He will have to decide whether to give a lecture, or to use a film or television broadcast, or whether to encourage his pupils to obtain their knowledge from books, and he will have to plan how the work is best recorded. I hope these few examples illustrate the complexity of presentation. Unfortunately, more consideration is generally given to this aspect of teaching in primary schools than on the secondary level. There are, I think, a number of reasons for this, but I sometimes wonder to what extent our present difficulties in secondary schools are connected with the lack of attention given to this aspect of teaching. This will be discussed in greater detail later.

So complex a task can, of course, not be executed perfectly all the time, nor can one plan for every contingency. One's judgment is not always correct either. In spite of more careful planning one can find oneself in most difficult situations. For example, during the war I was studying cavemen with a group of 5–7-year-olds. The children had made up a play and we had tried to find some material to make cavemen's skirts. Material was difficult to find. All cloth was rationed and paper was scarce. To our great delight an aunt of one of the girls was able to provide some cheap brown paper for that purpose. I had thought that the children would be able to cut five pieces each and, in caveman fashion, lace them together with string. The lesson went according to plan until it came to the lacing. I had not realised that most children of that age cannot lace. In fact only two of the twenty-five children in that group could do the lacing. With each of the children being surrounded by five pieces of rattling cheap brown paper and with twenty-three of them hankering after help, it was a rather harassing experience. Yet with the help of the two children who were able to do the lacing we achieved our aim and each child finished his or her skirt. The children were noisy, of course, but nothing disastrous happened. Conditions were, of course, favourable. The group was comparatively small, the children were fairly well-adjusted, we knew each other well and they were interested in what they were doing. I was also working in a school in which a certain amount of noise was tolerated. So I did not have the added anxiety that I might have lost class control. In less favourable circumstances this might easily have happened.

The complexities of keeping discipline

In my opinion the appropriateness of the subject matter and the presentation are very relevant to the ease with which a class can be controlled. Some of the complexities of keeping discipline in one's lessons were already mentioned when we considered the relationships within the classroom in terms of group dynamics. Considering the dependency of the group on the leader, pupils who are interested in their lessons and who find the tasks meaningful will naturally be more amenable to control. However, with the complexity of presentation and selection of the appropriate subject matter, one would expect frequent difficulties such as the one I experienced with the group of 5–7-year-olds. If one then considers the difficulties of controlling a large group in terms of the intensity of feelings, and particularly unacceptable feelings, expressed it does not seem surprising that class control is a matter of considerable concern to a teacher.

Yet this area of the teacher's work is hardly ever openly discussed. It is permissible for teachers-in-training and young inexperienced teachers to be worried about it as a survey conducted at Leicester (Tibble, 1959) indicates, but an experienced teacher expects to be able to control his class to perfection all the time. Some of them do up to a point. Most of them learn to keep their class quiet, because excessive noise is often thought to be a sign of a class out of control. Some teachers become more concerned with keeping their class quiet than with the learning task. As each teacher expects such perfection of himself, he cannot, of course, share his problems with his colleagues. This in turn increases the teacher's anxieties. The intensity of the stress, of course, varies from teacher to teacher, according to his skill and personality. Nevertheless, I think that the exhaustion felt by most teachers at the end of term is more closely linked to the demands made on the skills and personality of a teacher in keeping discipline over the children he teaches than to any other aspect of his work.

The importance of relationships within the staff group and between the staff and the school's management group

The intensity of the stress also depends on the relationship between each teacher and his colleagues and between the staff group and the school's management group, i.e. the head, deputy head, the heads of departments, and so on.

Schools are very complex institutions. The complexity is clearly demonstrated in Richardson's (1973) detailed account of her work as a consultant to one comprehensive school. The roles and responsibilities of those who work in a school are, of course, constantly in a state of change. Yet it is possible to make some generalisations.

For instance, the atmosphere, the morale and the relationship between the members of staff are generally very dependent on the personality, skills and preferences of the head of the school. The 'boss' is, of course, important in all institutions, but heads of schools in this country seem to be far more autonomous than directors of many other institutions. In a pilot study conducted for the Plowden Report (Caspari, 1965), I found that heads were entirely responsible for the management of the school, although they delegated responsibilities of management to other members of their staff. In the larger schools these delegations were generally linked to special positions, such as deputy head, heads of departments and tutors. In the small primary schools, however, some class teachers carried as much managerial responsibility as the deputy head.

The importance of the communication system

Similarly, the communication system in each school is largely dependent on the head's preferences. Observation suggests that it is up to him to decide what meetings are called, how matters of concern to the staff are communicated and whether or not staff members are consulted before decisions are made. Schools vary greatly in this respect, but even if staff consultation is fairly general, most decisions cannot be made without the head's consent.

It therefore stands to reason that the degree to which teachers will be able to discuss problems they meet in the classroom with the head and with other members of staff will greatly depend on the way in which the head encourages such discussion. In some schools such problems are discussed in staff meetings, or in meetings with the teachers of a year-group, or individually between a member of staff and the head or the head of department. In other schools, problems are only discussed in secret, between members of staff who trust each other. Sometimes they are not discussed at all. To this extent the degree of stress felt by each teacher in a school is closely linked to the head, and to the way in which he organises his school.

Teachers and parents

The teacher's worries about class control and about the effectiveness of his teaching are closely related to his relationship with the parents of his pupils. The Plowden Report on children in primary schools (DES, 1967) showed very clearly that there is often very little meaningful contact between parents and teachers. A number of ways were suggested to alter this situation, but effectively there has not been much change. Parent–teacher associations can be arranged, meetings can be called, but fruitful interaction between people can only occur when people feel secure.

Richardson (1973) makes a number of interesting suggestions why parents and teachers do not trust each other, although they are linked by their common interest in the child and usually express great desire for more contact. Richardson attributes this phenomenon to strong feelings of ambivalence on both sides, each of them unconsciously projecting both positive and negative sides of himself onto the other. This is a very complicated process. For instance, the teacher will identify with the loving aspects of the parents' role, but he may see the parents as reactionary, not so much because of the parents' behaviour, but because he, the teacher, does not like to acknowledge the reactionary side of himself. Similarly, the parents may identify with the teacher in respect of his giving the child an opportunity to use his cleverness, yet he may see the teacher as hostile not so much because the teacher rejects the child, but because the parent finds it difficult to acknowledge his own unconscious hostility to his child and therefore interprets the child's reports on the teacher in that way. This process of 'splitting', as it is called, is a very effective, entirely unconscious mechanism by which uncomfortable feelings can be avoided. However, it is obvious that it makes relationships rather difficult.

In my opinion, there are a number of other factors contributing to the difficulties. There is, for instance, the link between success in school and career choice in later life. Naturally parents are far more aware of this than their children. With the absence of clear criteria for his effectiveness, the teacher also wants the child to be successful. If things do not go as well as either parents or teachers expect, it is unavoidable that both are inclined to blame each other. The parents will doubt the teacher's skill in teaching, and the teacher will attribute the child's failure to the parents' attitudes at home. There is, of course, always some justification for these feelings. Neither teachers nor parents are perfect. Some parents and teachers can, of course, look at the problems much more realistically than others. In some cases it is also clear that there are some very obvious handicaps that prevent the child from being a success. Nevertheless, in the despair of realising that the child might not be as successful as both parents and teachers would wish, it is very human to blame each other.

The same mechanism applies to the child's behaviour. If he is naughty at school, the parents often think that the teacher is not strict enough, while the teacher attributes the child's difficulties to the excessive leniency or neglect at home. In this case, it is, I think, even more difficult for parents and teachers to be realistic. After all, the parents' influence on the development of their child is greatly diminished when they send him off to school at the age of 5. They are compelled to do this by law. The choice of school is limited for most parents and the length of the school day is generally at least seven hours even for young children.

The expectation of perfection in teachers

Most parents express relief when their child enters school. It relieves the mother from a great deal of work. It might even enable her to contribute more easily to the family's budget. Yet there is, I think, also a very strong feeling of regret and concern lest the child be unhappy or come to harm without the parents being able to come to his help. Naturally they will expect the teacher to take their place. They will also expect that the teacher will be at least as effective as they are. Often they will expect him to be almost an ideal extension of themselves. They will also expect him, as an expert, to be more effective in curbing the child's undesirable behaviour, to be just and fair, never angry, never ruffled and able to deal with all contingencies in an ideal way. Of course no parent would describe his expectations in these terms. Nevertheless, I think it is as reasonable for parents to expect this kind of expertise from the teacher as it is for a patient to expect his doctor to cure his illness. In both cases, everybody knows that this will not always be so, yet this realisation does not seem to influence the expectations.

In so far as the teacher is trained and can therefore be regarded as an expert in education, parents' expectation of his greater skills in handling their child seems entirely justified. Yet, when one considers that the teacher has constantly to deal with their child as a member of a large group, one realises that even with the greatest skill no teacher would be able to treat any child in this ideal way all the time. To this extent parents are constantly disappointed. Similarly, no doctor is able to cure all illness. He is well aware of it, and one of the most difficult aspects of his work is to convey this fact to his patients.

The consequences of these unrealistic expectations

Teachers also know their limitations, but in some ways that are difficult to explain they find it much more difficult to admit this, not only to other people, but also to themselves. As a teacher I always felt anxious and worried if things went wrong, particularly at the beginning of my career. I tried my utmost to keep it a secret. I soon learned that the head and my colleagues suspected trouble only if my class was noisy. So I learned to keep them quiet. I also realised that the children themselves rarely reported at home what had happened at school. They do sometimes, of course, particularly when they think they can induce their parents to complain about the teacher. Now, as a psychologist, I do not relish failure either. I worry if a patient does not turn up, if a child is untestable, if a boy whom I have helped to learn to read becomes delinquent. I wonder whether I could have done something about it. I wish I had not said this or that, or had not taken such and such action. I do not necessarily discuss my problems with my colleagues, but often I do, and I do not feel that I must keep my failures secret. I know that my colleagues are likely to be supportive rather than critical.

As a young teacher I felt that the head and the other members of staff expected me to be perfect. When I share these feelings with teachers now, they usually agree. Putting it in these terms they also agree that these expectations are entirely unrealistic, yet the head, the more experienced colleagues, tutors of training colleges, all the people in authority seem to encourage these expectations of such omnipotent skills. It is difficult to explain why this should be so. Teachers are generally very reasonable and tolerant people. May it be that they, too, identify with the parents? After all, they are the parents of their own children—or at least potentially parents—and expect from the teacher of their children what the parents of their pupils expect from them.

It is, I think, obvious that the stresses on the teacher must be considerable, if he feels that he constantly disappoints the expectations of the parents and those in authority. Yet most parents are also reasonable people, so one would expect that these stresses could be greatly reduced if parents and teachers could talk to each other about it. This does in fact sometimes happen, particularly in a school where the more experienced teachers can admit to failure. This was very noticeable in some of the meetings I had with the staff of some schools where we met to discuss a difficult child. As the explicit purpose of the meeting was to unravel between us some of the reasons for the child's undesirable behaviour there was an unspoken acceptance of the teacher's difficulties, and thus the teachers could share their problems with each other.

Yet I have rarely found that teachers can discuss their problems of control with the parents, particularly when the child's reaction to the teacher's behaviour shows some distress, as would be natural if the child had been punished. Again, one wonders why this should be so, when it is well known that parents, too, feel anxious about the effect of their behaviour on their children. They too have to punish their children at times. Perhaps parents would rather not know. From their own experience parents know that social training such as toilet training, personal hygiene, table manners and so on, are a rather unpleasant area of the educative process. It necessitates in varying degrees a restriction of the child's impulses in the interest of the community. It is frequently reinforced by reward and punishment. Perhaps parents are glad that much of this training is now carried out in school? Perhaps they do not wish to know of the pain that the child experiences at school? Perhaps the teacher does not want to tell the parents? After all, like all human beings, teachers, too, want to be loved. They are also afraid that the parents doubt their concern for the child if they find out that the child has to suffer. Perhaps the parents welcome the opportunity of identifying with the child's resentment of the teacher rather than to have to share with the teacher the responsibility for the child's resentment. For no child can like the adult who punishes him, at least at the moment when punishment is meted out.

This 'splitting' between home and school contributes more to keeping teachers and parents apart than is often realised. For children spend most of their waking hours at school, even at a very early age. When they are older the average child spends an additional 1-3 hours each night doing homework, with the result that for many adolescents, waking life is almost exclusively connected with school activities, except for weekends.

The need to reduce the stress

When we considered stresses on the child originating from the school situation, it became clear that adjustment to the problems was well within the capability of most children, and that this adjustment was beneficial to the development of the child. In considering the stresses that school life imposes on teachers, I am not so sure whether these challenges do not sometimes diminish the teacher's effectiveness. Challenges in the classroom in connection with the learning/teaching situation and class-control are unavoidable. By overcoming these challenges the teacher greatly increases his skill. However, his worries about his own effectiveness, his tendency to keep his problems away from his colleagues, the difficulty in sharing his concern with the parents, are in my opinion, counter-productive.

There are, of course, many ways by which these problems can be alleviated. In many schools ways have been found to share the problems. Similarly, there are many schools in which there is a very good relationship between teachers and parents. Yet it is never easy to identify why these problems bedevil one school and are almost absent in others. Usually all depends on the communication system the head establishes in his school, both between himself and his staff, and between himself and the parents. Much depends on the extent to which he is eager and able to understand the problems of both staff and parents, to what extent he is able to contain their worries and anxieties, particularly if they are linked, as they often are, to some implied criticism of the institution he runs. For just as the teacher feels that his teaching must be perfect, many heads also want to be seen to run a 'perfect' school.

Of course, all professionals have to come to terms with these stresses inherent in their profession. This is true of doctors, lawyers, nurses, social workers, scientists and so on, as much as it is of teachers. Yet the more they can be relieved of some of the stresses we mentioned the more effective their influence on the next generation will be. For this reason it is, I think, of the utmost importance to find ways and means to reduce the stress.

Part Two

The difficult child in the classroom

4
What is a difficult child?

So far the discussion has centred on difficulties arising
from the setting in which school life takes place, and on
the effect of this setting on the interaction of the people
who live and work in it. For instance, we have looked at
the organisation of school into classes and have examined
the effect of this setting on the feelings of the teachers and
the pupils and on the relationship between them. We have
talked about the relationship between the staff of a school
and its effect on the behaviour of each individual teacher
and the children he teaches. We have also examined some
of the seemingly irrational phenomena in this situation.
So far, however, we have omitted to consider those factors
that each individual child brings to this situation: his own
set of values, his expectations, and his past experiences.
These, too, contribute to the functioning of a school class
and may cause the behaviour of any one person within the
setting to differ greatly from what one might reasonably
expect. Naturally some types of behaviour difficulties cause
more concern than others. Some rebels in some classes are
much more difficult to deal with than other rebels in other
classes. Similarly, some teachers seem to experience more
disruptive behaviour than others.

In this part of the book I should like to discuss those
children whose behaviour is so different from that of
other children that they present serious problems to the
teacher and to their peers. These children are often called

'maladjusted'. This is a useful term to the extent to which it implies a problem of adjustment in relation to the demands that the social structure makes on them. To that extent problems of 'maladjustment' can be alleviated not only by changes in the maladjusted child, but also by changes in the setting. For instance, if a child is constantly disturbing in class because of his need for having the teacher to himself, his disturbing behaviour would disappear if he were taught in the one-to-one relationship with the teacher. Whether or not this would be of help to the child is another question. My preference for the term 'difficult' to describe these children is mainly due to the frequent use of the term 'maladjustment' exclusively for anti-social behaviour and I should like to include a wider range of difficulties such as severe learning problems or excessive shyness. Whatever term is used, it refers to those children whose behaviour is disturbing over a fairly long period of time and to a fairly large degree. In this respect they need to be distinguished from those children we discussed earlier, those who show difficulties due to more temporary upheavals, such as illness of one of the parents or the leaving of a beloved teacher. We know it is not easy to distinguish between these two groups; as the classroom situation itself is anxiety-arousing, problems can appear very easily, and in an anxiety-arousing situation many people might behave in seemingly unreasonable ways. Similarly, the classroom situation makes considerable demands on the children, and situations that demand a high degree of adjustment will more easily give rise to difficult behaviour. The teacher's expectation to deal with every child 'perfectly' all the time adds another complication.

Problems of identification

Often teachers blame themselves for the children's difficulties and are afraid that the children's behaviour is due to their own lack of skill, and that other people, such as the head, their more experienced colleagues or the parents may think so. These fears are frequently justified. Heads, colleagues and parents are often very critical and a more skilful teacher can often contain a difficult child who presents insuperable problems to another. Yet such fears frequently prevent teachers from observing the child more closely and from asking for help. For instance, in some schools a child is only brought to the attention of the educational psychologist when there is a crisis. When the head, the teacher and the psychologist try to unravel the problem it becomes evident that the child has been difficult over a very long time. However, his difficulties could not be discussed until it was quite clear to the staff of the school that they were not due to failure of teaching skills.

Not long ago, for instance, Paul, aged 12, was brought to my attention because he had been involved in an incident in which a football had mysteriously disappeared. It had been found in his locker but nobody could find out how it got there. There was some evidence that Paul had taken it, but Paul denied it fervently. When Paul was discussed, it emerged that this incident was of fairly small importance in comparison with other aspects of his behaviour. For a long time the teachers had been worried about Paul, who did no work whatsoever and generally appeared to be disgruntled and sulky. Only when the football disappeared could the teachers bring themselves to look at Paul as a difficult child, partly, I think, because the incident took place outside the classroom situation and was not related to teaching.

Again there are no hard and fast rules by which 'difficult' children can be detected with certainty. Yet I often wish they could be identified earlier, for the sooner a child can be helped the more effective this help is likely to be. By and large there are more therapeutic facilities for younger children than for older ones. Some teachers are extraordinarily skilful in detecting these 'difficult' children

41

and some schools are extraordinarily good at helping them.

Identification of these children naturally grows with experience. Once one has spotted Johnny's special difficulty and seen Jimmy behave in a similar way, Jimmy's problem will be more easily understood. Yet Jimmy's problems will also be different from Johnny's. Therefore, a description of difficult behaviour can only give the reader a general idea. The children I am going to describe will never be exactly like any particular difficult child one knows, but I hope that some of the common characteristics will become apparent.

Choice of cases

I shall choose mainly children who were referred to me by teachers and about whom enough information was accumulated to find some links between their 'difficult' behaviour in school and the conflict in themselves that caused this behaviour. These links are much more difficult to find than is often thought. For instance, if teachers learn that a difficult child comes from a broken home, they often assume that the child's home conditions are the cause of such behaviour at school. This is, of course, very frequently the case, but often there are other much more subtle and much more important factors contributing to the disturbance. Sometimes these more subtle factors remain obscure for lack of information. This does not necessarily prevent us from giving these children very substantial help, but one's understanding increases primarily by realising what links there might be and by learning that one can only find these links by very minute and skilful detective work, by careful and objective observation of the child and by seeking information from all the sources available, such as school records, observations of other teachers, from parents, social workers, or the child guidance team.

Categories of difficulties

It is not easy to categorise these 'difficult' children, nor does a child belong exclusively to one group. In fact, most difficult children show a number of behaviour difficulties either simultaneously or at various times. The Isle of Wight study (Rutter, 1970) gives many examples of this kind. Yet to facilitate discussion about the main characteristics of the behaviour of difficult children, grouping is unavoidable.

I have chosen five fairly comprehensive categories: the child with behaviour problems, the child with learning problems, the withdrawn or over-docile child, the school refuser and the delinquent child. These categories refer to difficulties manifested in a school setting, with the exclusion of those that more frequently show at home. The groupings overlap; for instance, both the school refusers and the delinquent children are also children with behaviour problems. However, they form special sub-groups presenting special problems and demanding special consideration.

In each category I shall give a description of the children's typical behaviour in school and I shall illustrate these with case histories. I shall attempt to describe the children's behaviour as it was observed so that the reader can make up his own mind whether the links between the child's behaviour and the disturbance is justified.

Finally, whenever possible, I shall relate the child's behaviour to his home conditions, and to his early childhood experience to indicate some of the underlying conflicts that may have contributed to his difficulties.

5
The child with behaviour problems

Irrespective of the seriousness of a child's emotional disturbance, teachers naturally worry most about those children who show difficulties in learning and those that have behaviour problems, as problems in these areas can be most easily linked to the teacher's skills. Generally they are more concerned about behaviour difficulties than about their pupil's cognitive failure. There are a number of reasons for this. For instance, a child with behaviour difficulties can easily disturb the educational progress of other children, while children who cannot learn will only hamper their own. Moreover, there is general recognition that children function on different levels intellectually while one expects conforming behaviour in all children. If a child cannot learn, one can always assume that there is a lack of intellectual endowment. If necessary, an objective measure can be obtained via an intelligence test. However, there is no recognised measure to show that a child is unable to behave appropriately in class. Moreover, disturbing behaviour in adult society is often punished by law. Lack of academic success in school results usually only in restriction of career choice.

Peter, aged 9, for instance, was a child who was so difficult in class that he had to be excluded and would spend day after day in the secretary's office. Under these circumstances Peter did not learn very much. By the time he was 10 his behaviour had improved to such a degree that he could be contained in class. The teacher was delighted about this change. She was so concerned about controlling him that she only gave him easy work to do. Whenever he found anything difficult he objected and she allowed him to discontinue with his tasks, because she was afraid that he would become difficult to handle. In this way Peter only improved to the extent that he could pick up knowledge by himself. To my mind, the teacher's attitude was entirely justified. Peter's difficult behaviour would have disturbed all the other children and might have wrecked the lesson. In this way Peter did not make much progress, but other children were able to learn.

Main characteristics

The behaviour patterns of children with behaviour problems are not easy to summarise. The difference between them and ordinary naughty children is mainly a matter of degree. However, they show some general characteristics by which they can be identified. For instance, the behaviour of ordinary children can be modified by reward and punishment, reasoning or heart-to-heart talks. Children with behaviour problems persist with their unacceptable behaviour, in spite of rewards or punishment. They promise to change, but they never do. They often show aggressive defiance of the teacher at the slightest provocation; they are inclined to regard punishment as unfair, even if the evidence shows clearly that they were to blame. They frequently use bad language. They are untrustworthy, sly and often tell lies. They are unpopular and do not keep a friend for long. They are spiteful to other children and fight and bully them. They spoil or hide other children's work. The way they behave leads one to feel that they intend to be objectionable and this often arouses great antagonism in the teacher. The child's action seems deliberate. It is often hard to accept that the child can actually do nothing to control his behaviour. He almost wants to

45

make the teacher angry so that he will be punished and he will continue to be difficult until he has reached this goal. Then he usually complains or cries bitterly.

Of course, no child shows all these symptoms. Age also makes a considerable difference. In an infant school one would find such children to be hyperactive and inclined to throw temper tantrums. They are also inclined to wander around the school. Secondary school children are more likely to fight with their peers or be rude to the teacher, defy school rules, or damage school property.

The story of *Alan*

Let me give some examples: Alan was 6 when he was first referred to me. He was a little coloured boy, half West African and half English. He was an illegitimate child who had grown up in a children's home from birth. He was referred for temper tantrums. This meant that at various times he would throw himself on the floor and scream, usually when he felt frustrated about something. He also could not read, nor could he do any sums. He often interfered with other people's work and fought with other children. The teachers did not mention this at first. They only talked of his screaming. They were bothered by his fighting and his lack of competence, but I do not think that they would have referred him for this. They were sure that his temper tantrums were something out of the ordinary.

The teachers were, of course, quite right. Psychological investigations and interviews with the psychiatrist revealed a great many conflicts and difficulties.

Alan was given psychotherapy and educational therapy and we were able to keep in touch with him and his teachers until he was 13 years old. As he grew up his temper tantrums disappeared but he continued to be difficult to control. He also found it extremely difficult to learn. Although his various teachers found ways and means of dealing with his behaviour, every teacher I talked to over the years found him one of the most difficult children in his or her class. After the initial referral his misdemeanours were rarely excessive, but he was a constant irritant. He often did not follow instructions. He pushed his peers when lining up before leaving the classroom. He lost his books and covered them with ink. He could also be very affectionate and he was genuinely sorry for what he had done at the time. This did not prevent him from doing it again on the next occasion. While he was in treatment with us he began to visit an aunt and uncle who eventually adopted him, and the last we heard of him was that he was doing very well.

The reaction of the various teachers over the years illustrates how difficult it is to understand this kind of behaviour. The infant school teachers had no doubt in their minds that Alan could not help himself. He screamed for reasons that he could not control. When, a year later, he exhibited the same behaviour in the junior school, the teacher punished him severely and was very pleased with herself that he had not screamed since. She had been told of his difficult behaviour before he came to her class. She thought that she might have 'cured' him. She only began to realise that his difficulties were beyond his control when, the following term, he viciously scratched another boy's face. She could accept the link between the screaming then and the aggression towards the other child now. As Alan grew older his behaviour became far less dramatic and teachers found it more and more difficult to accept that he was not entirely responsible for his naughty behaviour. When he was about 10, for instance, he upset a lot of ink over the classroom floor. To some degree it looked like an accident, but the details of the incident led one to believe that there was something purposeful in it as well. Yet it was difficult to pinpoint to what extent Alan had really spilt the ink on purpose, and to what extent his action was caused by conflicts of which he was not aware. It was

47

easier to understand this when his behaviour was very strikingly unusual, e.g. when he screamed at the age of 6. This was far more difficult to appreciate when his behaviour was only just annoying.

Why did Alan scream? Why was he so difficult? Although he had been in a good children's home, he was crying out for love and affection. We know little of his early life, but we know that he changed his home at the age of 5. One wonders what this change meant to him. As in most children's homes the house-parents change from time to time, so Alan had never known any 'permanent' adult who cared for him. His colour was also a problem to him. He wanted to be accepted however bad he was. Like many institutionalised children he felt he was very bad indeed. Did his own parents reject him because of his badness? Did the house-parents change because of his unbearable behaviour? He was unable to express these problems directly, but some of them emerged from his drawings and stories. As he experienced the permanent affection of his 'aunt' and 'uncle' and the regular treatment at the clinic, he began to be able to accept the demands of the classroom situation. With extra help he began to learn. By the time he was adopted he was able to control his feelings. There are many children like Alan in children's homes.

Daniel and his problems with aggression

Nine-year-old Daniel was to some degree even more troublesome at school than Alan. His parents were well off, but they were divorced. Daniel was in the habit of pushing children for no apparent reason, and on one occasion he scratched a girl's leg with a cocktail stick until it bled. Mothers of other children complained about him to the teacher and objected to their children sitting next to Daniel. In spite of this very objectionable behaviour, the teacher reported that there was something very appealing about Daniel, when she talked to him and reprimanded him.

Daniel was also a problem at home. There was a close connection between his home circumstances and his behaviour at school. He lived with his mother and a younger brother with whom Daniel quarrelled all the time. Mother preferred the brother, who was much better behaved at home and much more successful at school than Daniel. The mother tried not to favour her younger son, but she was aware of her preferences.

It seemed very obvious that Daniel's attacks on other children at school were connected with his jealousy of his younger brother. He attacked his brother at home, just as he attacked the children at school. His attacks on his brother were, of course, linked to his feelings of being unwanted and unloved at home. They also ensured that his mother took notice of him. Similarly, his attacks on the other children at school necessitated the teacher's attention. Once he had the teacher's attention, e.g. when she talked to him, he could be very appealing. Just as his frequent quarrels with his younger brother can be seen as his way of telling his mother that he felt hurt by her preference of the younger child, he showed his teacher how hurt he was by her attending to other children. Neither the mother nor the teacher neglected him. Neither of them could give him as much attention as he desired. The reasons for Daniel's insatiable greed for attention were very complex and complicated and not easy to discover.

Daniel's attention-seeking behaviour made the teacher's life very difficult. She understood that he wanted attention and that he needed it, yet as one of forty children he could not get what he wanted. She also had to protect the other children from his attacks. So she had to reprimand him and punish him, just as his mother did at home. In this way Daniel was caught in a vicious circle which was difficult to break. He wanted to be loved, he felt angry because he could not get what he wanted, he attacked other children because he was angry, and therefore could not get the love he wanted. Daniel was helped very effectively by weekly psychotherapy in a setting where his mother could also talk to someone about her problems.

Conrad and his uncontrollable temper tantrums

Conrad's behaviour caused his teachers problems in a slightly different way. He was 13 when he was referred for attacking a teacher. He had to be held by two other teachers and two prefects to prevent him from carrying out his attack. This kind of uncontrolled behaviour left no doubt in the teacher's mind that he was unable to control his feelings. He was a very strong boy. As he grew a little older his behaviour was no longer so dramatic. He no longer attacked adults, but he was rude to them and used very bad language. He fought with other children. He jumped the wall of the school in school hours in order to buy sweets. He created disturbances in class. He was frequently caned for his misdemeanours but showed no improvement. He was very defiant whenever he was caught breaking the school rules. His house-master was adamant that Conrad knew what he was doing and to some extent this was so.

On one occasion, however, Conrad had to be caned by the house-master for a certain misdemeanour. He received the caning and then returned to receive a second caning for the same misdeed. This was again so unusual that the house-master could accept that Conrad's behaviour was odd. In fact the pattern of behaviour over a considerable time indicated that Conrad's objectionable behaviour was linked to a desire to be caned.

Conrad, it seemed, wanted to be relieved of his feelings of guilt. By being referred for caning Conrad could also obtain the personal attention of the house-master whom he liked very much. This caning also brought him into physical contact with this teacher, and it was probably very important for him to have contact and 'care' on such a primitive level. Conrad, therefore, sought out the punishment that was meant to be a deterrent and only when his behaviour became very odd was the teacher able to understand it. Even so, it needed very careful observation.

Knowledge of Conrad's home background also helped in understanding why he behaved in such an unusual way.

Conrad was a West Indian whose mother left the West Indies when the child was 6 years old. He must have been quite difficult even then, because his aunt, who was looking after him, wrote to his mother saying that she could no longer keep him because he was too difficult to manage. He came to England at the age of 10 by aeroplane, dropping out of the sky and unable to recognise his mother when he arrived. His mother said that she could not recognise him either. Conrad's younger sister had come to England the previous year and there was now another little baby brother. Mother was not married to his father, but had lived with him ever since Conrad was born. We were never able to find out why mother could not make up her mind to marry the children's father, but it became very clear that Conrad was in many ways expected to take over some of father's responsibilities. He was supposed to look after the children when mother was not there. He was supposed to do the washing up. He was also very often left at home when the rest of the family went out, apparently because he had nothing to wear. He had plenty of reasons for being angry with his father, his mother, his brother and sister and the world in general. He often felt rejected by everyone in the family.

His West Indian background and attitude towards authority did not help matters either. Although he often misbehaved because he unconsciously sought punishment, as we have seen, he made it very clear that in his opinion there was nothing wrong with breaking rules, particularly when he was caught by a teacher he did not know. In his view the only thing to do when caught red-handed, was to persuade the teacher that he had not done it, irrespective of the evidence. He talked about this in a very matter-of-fact way, as if this was the accepted philosophy of those with whom he lived. Other West Indian children I know have expressed similar views.

Conrad's attitude to law and order is very typical of children who break rules. Consciously they only see the connection between their being caught and their being punished, and not between the punishment and the crime. They are not aware that they seek the punishment. This tendency is only betrayed by their action. They often flaunt the rules so openly that they are bound to be caught, or they behave in seemingly inappropriate ways, like Conrad, who wanted to be caned twice. Although this link between Conrad's behaviour at school and his home background gave some understanding of the causes for this behaviour, basically it did not help his teachers in dealing with him. It was, of course, very important to recognise why Conrad wanted to make his teachers angry, why he wanted to be punished, but this did not give them any guidelines as to how to help him to conform more readily.

There is, to my mind, no definite answer as to how such children can be handled. Every teacher does it in his or her own way. Yet if the teacher recognises that a child's difficult behaviour has nothing directly to do with him, he ceases to blame himself for the child's difficult behaviour and can often deal with him much more effectively than he was previously able to do. It is difficult to pinpoint what is happening. To an outsider it merely seems that the child is less of a problem. Of course, the behaviour of some children is so difficult that a teacher or an institution cannot contain them, and often the best help can be given if the teacher or the school can accept this without shame or embarrassment.

The story of Dick

Dick, for instance, was helped greatly by his headmaster's decision to exclude him from school, a decision that the headmaster found very difficult to make. Dick had originally been referred by his junior school for temper tantrums. He was 8 at that time. He was also very spiteful to other children. He had few friends and complained bitterly when other children reacted to his spiteful behaviour by attacking him. He told lies about others and complained constantly that he was blamed unfairly. It was not difficult to find some of the underlying factors that contributed to Dick's difficult behaviour. His father had been in prison several times. One brother was in a community school and another was in a boarding-school for maladjusted children. Other siblings were also difficult in school and at home. There was very little money. Both father and mother had had previous marriage partners and there was a lot of conflict between the parents.

Investigations at the Child Guidance Clinic gave the impression that Dick was only able to make shallow relationships, that he felt the world was against him and that he found it very difficult to have any positive feelings towards anyone. All this did not help the school in handling Dick, but it did help us to come to the conclusion that the best way of helping Dick would be to place him in a residential school for maladjusted children to give him a chance to find adults to whom he could safely attach himself. This was done and Dick's capacity to make relationships increased considerably. He became more in touch with his feelings, but he still found it very difficult to express these and one was not quite sure how much had gone underground and how much Dick was showing. He had been placed in a primary school for maladjusted children and there was no secondary residential school that he could go to. He had also expressed a wish to live at home. At the age of 11 he was therefore placed in a local comprehensive school for a trial period. He was allocated to the remedial class of the school with a very understanding teacher, and his progress and behaviour were so acceptable that the headmaster and the teachers decided to keep him on. So Dick remained at the secondary school for a year.

At the end of that year Dick's teacher left. He again became unruly and he threatened to jump out of the top-floor window. He hated the deputy head and was quite unmanageable. He no longer did any work in school.

At this point I discussed Dick with his headmaster who felt that the school had failed Dick. However, in consideration of Dick's background the headmaster could be helped to understand that this was not so, that in Dick's interest he should be placed in a day school for maladjusted children and that he should be suspended from school, as his behaviour caused such anxiety to so many children and staff members.

This was done. In his new school Dick's behaviour deteriorated at first. In an atmosphere where acting out was permitted, Dick became more unruly and difficult to handle than he had ever been before. However, in an institution especially designed to make allowances for such behaviour and with the help of the very skilful headmistress he was able to experience the kind of relationship with adults that he really needed, i.e. a relationship in which much of his unruly behaviour could be accepted. It was the turning point in Dick's life. From then onwards he became far more capable of coping with school work and life in general.

Dick's story highlights two other points that need to be kept in mind when handling children with behaviour problems: the headmaster of the comprehensive school considered the other children and the staff of the school as well as Dick. He also realised that Dick could not be helped within the setting of a large comprehensive school. He was able to make a realistic appraisal of the effect of this child's behaviour on the rest of the community and of his school's suitability to give effective help. This is of the utmost importance. It is not at all easy to make objective judgments in these areas. One school might be able to contain a particular child, while a similar child could not possibly be helped in another school.

Roland and his headmistress

Roland, aged 8, for instance, could be helped in his ordinary primary school by his headmistress. When Roland had come to the junior school he attacked the teacher and threw books around the classroom whenever the teacher was trying to settle him down to work. The school was in an educationally deprived area and there were many children with behaviour difficulties, so the teacher dealt with Roland as well as she could. He was brought to my attention when the teacher had found him jabbing a child with a knife, and holding a little girl up by her hair in the playground. At the same time Roland's behaviour had also deteriorated. The headmistress reported that Roland was sent to her constantly and that she could not contain him any longer in school. She did in fact suspend him for a few days. He was referred to the clinic for an assessment, and it was recommended that he should be placed in a day school for maladjusted children. However, there was no vacancy and in the meantime the headmistress of his primary school had found ways to deal with him. She had established a very good relationship with him and had been able to accept his aggressive feelings when they were expressed in socially acceptable ways. For instance, on one occasion when Roland had been very aggressive towards a younger child, the headmistress had talked to him about the necessity for control particularly in relationship to younger children and referred to the police as an example. Roland listened very attentively but replied that at this moment he was not feeling like a policeman.

He was feeling rather like a very nasty thief. The head-mistress was able to accept this statement and talked to him about his conflicts. In time Roland's difficulties diminished considerably. He remained in this primary school until his transfer to secondary school.

This example illustrates to what extent the child can be helped by the relationship he can make with one parti-cular person. In Roland's case the headmistress allocated time to talk to him every time that he needed her, over a period of about six months. She was also a very under-standing person and a person who was very concerned about this child. Not every head of a junior school is able to do this work. Not every head wants to do it. It would have been very difficult for a teacher to see Roland individually and also have him in her class. Roland would have found it unbearable to have to share her after seeing her alone. However, the headmistress did not teach Roland. She was, therefore, able to see him individually without causing any conflict.

Mary, the fire-raiser

Mary, aged 13, was another child who was helped by her school. She was brought to our attention because she had attempted to set the school on fire. She had been found in the cloakroom trying to light the curtains. She had been prevented from doing this and had subsequently been found doing the same thing in the girls' lavatory.

Mary came from a very difficult family. Mother fre-quently threatened to leave the family and did so from time to time for short periods. Father was often violent and one of the older brothers was in a remand home, for robbery. Mary was assessed at the clinic and was found to be a very depressed and anxious girl who found it difficult to cope within a group. She was able to function much better in a close relationship with an adult. The school medical officer had suggested to the school that she might go to a tutorial class, but the teachers thought they could help her themselves. Two members of the school staff decided to devote a good deal of time to Mary and with this additional attention Mary's behaviour improved. She began to feel much happier in school and she made progress in her school work. Again, the teachers were able to help because of the personal attention they could give to this girl.

The problems of helping these children

I hope that these examples give some illustration of the complexity of behaviour problems. Perhaps the only thing all these children had in common was their feeling of frustration and their need for love, and the way they tried to get what they wanted by their difficult behaviour, which inevitably led to disapproval. The examples also demonstrate how difficult it is for a teacher to be sure that the problem is in the child and is not due to his inability to keep him in order. The referral of each of the children quoted only happened after some very dramatic behaviour on the part of the child. Some of these children were in their teens, and teachers had put up with their difficult behaviour for years. Understandably, the teachers did not wish to draw attention to a difficult child if they were afraid that the behaviour of the child might be a reaction to the behaviour of the teacher.

From the child's point of view this is, of course, a great pity. Generally, the earlier the child receives help the more effective this help is likely to be. Sometimes help may no longer be available when he is older. If Dick had been a year or two older than he was, when his behaviour caused his suspension from the comprehensive school, hardly any day school for maladjusted children would have taken him. The staff of these schools rightly feel that they cannot help a child unless they have adequate time to do so. Yet, as long as the climate in schools is such that the teacher is afraid of being criticised if things go wrong, conditions are not likely to change.

Help for these children is not easy to obtain either. It can be seen from the examples that each child was helped in a slightly different way. The help offered often depends on what is available. The willingness of parents to involve themselves in treatment also plays an important part. Parents have to agree to the treatment of their children. They have to take the children to the Child Guidance Clinic. They can discontinue the treatment of their children if they wish to do so. Moreover, the change in a child, however beneficial to him, might cause the break-up of the stability of a family which would, of course, not be to his advantage in the long run.

Finally, let us admit that our knowledge of these behaviour disorders is still very much in its infancy. We could see in every one of these cases that the problems were linked to some factors in the child's home conditions, which were beyond the control of those who cared for him. We do not know, at present, how to prevent the occurrence of these problems. Perhaps we will never know, but as long as we are so much in the dark our remedies are bound to be haphazard. Yet our understanding of these children, even our desire to understand, will help because it will assist us in our reaction towards the children's behaviour, and this will be sufficient to reduce the problems of many children to manageable proportions. This happens more often than is generally believed, for teachers are as secretive about their successes as they are about their failures; both, I think, because of the insecurity inherent in the teacher's job.

6
Children with learning problems

Whatever philosophy a particular teacher holds, whether he sees the chief aim of the educational process as the acquisition of knowledge and skills or whether he aims to develop the whole personality, cognitive success is the only aspect of this educational process that can be evaluated quantitatively. Everybody knows that our lives have been greatly influenced by the understanding and help that we have received from some of our teachers during our school life. Our value system and our attitude to life are probably far more influenced by our teachers than we know. One need only ask an adult why he liked a particular subject. Generally the answer will be that he liked the teacher. Whether or not this is true is difficult to determine. However, there is no doubt that one's academic success at school had a profound influence on one's career, particularly that part of success that can be measured by examination results. Now that the 11-plus examination is fading out, examination results are, of course, often the more immediate concern of secondary school teachers. In secondary schools the status of a teacher is very frequently linked to the examination results of his pupils, although this is hardly ever made explicit. In particular parents value a teacher whose pupils consistently have had good results in public examinations. Similarly, they value an infant teacher whose pupils attain a high standard of reading. In either of these cases the means by which the high standard is reached is felt to be of only secondary importance. Whether the result is achieved because the children are enthusiastic about the learning or whether they are pressurised into doing the work very often matters only when a child shows definite signs of unhappiness. Many teachers are, of course, critical of this over-valuation of academic success.

Yet from a child's point of view, and from that of his parents, examination results are of enormous importance because of their consequences for the child's future. Morris (1966) states that a child whose reading age at 8 years is not at least equal to his chronological age is not likely to make use of the opportunities of our educational system. Similarly, the number of 'O' and 'A' levels obtained by an adolescent will determine the limits of his career choice. He will not be able to go to university unless he has passed three 'A' levels. He will not be able to enter the university of his choice unless he has passed these subjects at a fairly high level. Other occupations depend on the number of 'O' levels obtained and sometimes on 'O' levels in particular subjects. A child who cannot read is excluded from a large number of professions : he cannot become a postman, he would find it difficult to serve in a shop because he cannot write down the orders, he is even handicapped in getting about town if he cannot read the names of streets or underground and railway stations.

Teachers' attitudes to learning problems

Children with learning difficulties are therefore also a cause of much concern to teachers. Again, as I said before, the teacher cannot be sure whether the child's lack of success is due to the teacher's inability to arouse or keep his interest or whether the child's failure is the result of lack of ability, home circumstances or other factors which are clearly not under the teacher's control. Again, the teacher is reluctant to draw attention to a child who is failing to learn. This is particularly so at the beginning of a child's school life, when he is learning those skills that most people in western society can master, such as reading, writing and arithmetic. I have often met experienced infant school teachers who singled out children with severe learning problems at the age of 6. They were very willing to accept advice in helping them at school, but when I suggested that it might be wiser to refer them for a more thorough investigation they always demurred that the child will 'grow out of it'. They did not want to involve the parents unless they were quite certain that the child's lack of progress had nothing to do with them. Again one can well understand this attitude.

By the time children reach secondary school their rate of progress is, of course, expected to be more varied. Examination results are objective measures, and the teacher feels more secure. In some cases perhaps he does not worry enough. There have been a number of children who could hardly read at all and were referred for help just two terms before they left school. They were usually well behaved and their teachers thought they were learning until a more experienced teacher discovered them. The reasons for their failure were usually very complex.

Children have many different kinds of learning difficulties. Some affect the child's educational progress more seriously than others. Some suddenly appear and disappear with a minimum of help. Some are very fundamental to the child's personality and very difficult, sometimes almost impossible, to alleviate. Frequently it seems that the child is deliberately obstructing the teacher's attempts to help him to acquire knowledge and skills. For instance, teachers often feel that a child 'could do better if he made more effort'—a remark frequently occurring in school reports. The teacher's observation is usually correct. The child's work is often very untidy, very careless, unfinished, and very erratic. Sometimes he does excellent work and then again his work is very poor. Alternatively, the child might

61

do very good work in one subject and very bad work in another. It may be a passing phase due to temporary pre-occupations that goes as quickly as it has come. It may go on for months and years. It may have affected his ability to learn right from the beginning.

Sudden deterioration of work

The sudden occurrence of careless work seems to appear more frequently in adolescence than at any other time of a child's development. Norman, aged 14, for instance, got a very poor report because his homework was very badly done. Norman attended a grammar school and was a bright boy. He had been a very good pupil in the past, but now his homework was careless and untidy and he often omitted to give it in altogether.

He admitted that he preferred to spend a great deal of time after school with sprinting activities and often felt too tired to do his homework. He had very good reasons for this—he was a splendid athlete. In this case it was not very difficult to help Norman to make a compromise. He was able to organise himself so that he could practise running and do satisfactory homework as well and his school report improved.

Not many adolescents like Norman are referred for deterioration of work. Parents and teachers often feel that the youngster only has to 'pull himself together' and everything will be all right. If there is no change they feel that the more demanding work presents a genuine difficulty that the youngster is not able to overcome.

This is, of course, often the case. School work can easily deteriorate if the youngster is preoccupied with other things. We have seen this with the class of 15-year-old girls who directed their attention to having crushes on teachers at the expense of their school work. School work also increases in difficulty as the child grows older, and a child who previously succeeded by hard work can suddenly no longer keep up. The deterioration of Norman's work was so striking because he was such an intelligent boy, but deterioration of work can, of course, happen to children of all ability levels. Naturally, teachers and parents are most concerned about children of high ability. It is far more difficult to notice such deterioration if the child is not very bright to start with.

Although the symptoms look so simple, sudden deterioration of work may occur for very complex reasons, which may have nothing to do with school. To some extent this was true of Norman, too. During my interviews with Norman it became quite clear that his refusal to do homework was also a form of rebellion against his mother, although Norman was not aware of this. In this way Norman's work did not only improve because he was able to make a compromise. He might not have been able to keep this up if we had not been able to discuss the relationship with his mother as well, and if I had not been able to see his mother myself. This is, of course, difficult to prove. This experience only suggests that there may be other youngsters who could benefit by talking things over with someone else, e.g. with a school counsellor.

Joanna, aged 15, was helped in this way. She was a gifted child working for several 'O' level subjects, but was unable to pass examinations. All her teachers expected her to pass, but on two consecutive occasions she walked out of the examination room as she felt she could not answer any of the questions. Her problem appeared to be linked to a rather unreasonable feeling of guilt. She felt that she must not succeed because she had several brothers and sisters who were physically and mentally ill. She was quite aware of this, but insight did not help.

She also had a very disturbed mother, and father had died when she was quite young. The extent of her conflict became apparent when after failing one of her examinations, she took an overdose of barbiturates which she had taken away from her mother.

Joanna was helped by regular meetings with a counsellor, who was able to persuade her to seek the psychiatric help she needed.

Specific learning difficulties

Both Joanna and Norman were in their teens, but children can have difficulties in learning when they are quite young. Nicky, aged 6, for instance, could not learn because he could not sit still. He could never concentrate on any work, he could only listen to a story read by the teacher if he was sitting right next to her. He also belonged to the large group of children who, in spite of sufficient overall intelligence, find it almost impossible to learn what are generally called the 'basic subjects'.

Reading difficulties and behaviour problems

These specific learning difficulties occur mainly in reading, spelling and arithmetic and sometimes in all three of these subjects. The most serious of these is the inability to learn to read, because the lack of reading ability jeopardises educational success in the future more than any other cognitive weakness. The multitude of factors that can contribute to reading disability is very clearly and simply described by Ravenette (1968). Like Nicky, many of those children have behaviour problems as well, just as many of the children mentioned in the previous chapter had not learned to read. This link between behaviour disorders and reading disability is strong and, I think, one of the important findings of the Isle of Wight study (Rutter, 1970) mentioned earlier.

Evidence from a more detailed unpublished study of a much smaller sample supports Rutter's findings of this link. It was found that of 51 children with severe reading disability, 27 also showed signs of behaviour disorders and 7 of a group of 17 docile and rather withdrawn children became anti-social as they began to learn. The entire sample of 51 children showed great conflict in respect of their aggressive feelings, in their drawings and other expression work and in their projective tests. Conflict over aggressive feelings is, of course, one of the main difficulties linked to anti-social behaviour. It is also generally recognised that one has to be assertive in order to learn. We often use metaphors such as 'attacking a problem' or 'wrestling with a task' in connection with learning. What is not always accepted is the close link between assertiveness and aggression. Most teachers of young children find that some of those that have difficulty in learning are also naughty. They also know that some of their pleasant, complacent children do not make progress in learning and do not seem to try. They sometimes observe that some of these children become behaviour problems, but seldom link this phenomenon to progress in learning which has also taken place. It seems as if these docile, slightly withdrawn children are unable to learn because they feel that even the assertion necessary for learning is an aggressive action they have to avoid. Once they begin to read, they experience that it is safe to express these feelings, but then they express them indiscriminately, destructively as well as constructively and become anti-social.

One of the most outstanding examples is that of Arnold. He was 8 years old and could not read at all. When he was first given help the parents were contacted and mother was very keen to see a social worker, because there were many other problems of which she was aware. In the second interview mother was joined by father who pronounced that this was all nonsense, that Arnold had no problems whatsoever and that his reading disability was exclusively the school's fault. When I checked up with the headmistress of Arnold's school she confirmed that he was a very nice, well behaved little boy, whose only problem was that he could not learn to read. As Arnold continued with his lessons he began to learn. Three months later he was constantly involved in ferocious fights in the playground. Shortly afterwards he was taken to court for larceny which he had committed with a gang of other boys. Fortunately, such extreme, sudden changes are relatively rare.

Robert's aggressive feelings appeared in a much more acceptable way in his free writing. When he was referred he was 14 years old and could read a few words. He had been one of those boys who had been missed because of his amenable behaviour. I met him first when he came to secondary school. He was then 11 years old and could not read at all, but we had no vacancy to help him immediately. When I made enquiries a year later I was told by his teacher that extra help was no longer needed, as Robert had made great strides in reading. In his last year at school his class teacher, who was also a remedial teacher, spotted Robert's difficulty and referred him again. It was easy to see why he had been missed: he had a very good short-term memory, and he was able to read quite fluently at the end of a short period as long as the same words were frequently repeated. At the next occasion Robert no longer knew any of these words, but again he was much more fluent at the end of the lesson and gave the impression that he had made progress. Robert was a very likeable chap. He was slight and pale, but wiry and agile. He had many friends and was very popular with the teachers. His father was ill and his mother was a hard-working woman who looked after a large family as well as she could.

When Robert began to learn he was also encouraged to dictate stories. The last of these was a detective story about the murder of a girl, with a vivid account of a vicious fight between two young men, described very colourfully and with great fervour. By this time Robert had mastered all the simple phonic rules and was able to read on an 8-year-old level. He was able to express his aggressive feelings constructively in his stories, so his behaviour was not affected by his progress.

Physical defects and specific reading disability

Specific reading disability need not necessarily, of course, be due to psychological causes, such as those quoted above. Physical defects, particularly defects in vision and hearing, are often contributory factors and are sometimes extraordinarily difficult to discover. One of these is high frequency deafness. This is a hearing defect in respect of some consonant sounds only. Children with high frequency deafness often do not give the impression of being deaf. They are quite able to understand, often with the help of lip-reading. A slight speech defect such as a confusion between *d* and *th* might be an indication of high frequency deafness. Naturally such children find it very difficult to learn phonics. If one does not *hear* the difference between sounds, how is one expected to recognise them in print? The children themselves cannot, of course, report their condition, because like all children born with such deficits, they expect other people to be exactly like them. However, high frequency deafness can be diagnosed. There is even a very easy screening test (Reed, 1970) that a teacher could very well use. High frequency deafness is, however, difficult to remedy. Hearing aids for selective sounds are very expensive and those provided by the National Health Service increase the overall volume of sounds. Jonathan, aged 13, for instance, hardly ever used his hearing aid to the great despair of his teachers, who did not realise that the overall volume of sound was unbearable to him. They thought Jonathan refused to wear his hearing aid for reasons similar to those that cause children to refuse to wear glasses, viz. for fear of being ridiculed by their peers. Jonathan had learning as well as behaviour difficulties. He also had many other problems. It is difficult to judge to what extent these were linked to his high frequency deafness, but his emotional problems were exacerbated by his physical defect.

Adrian, aged 10, was another child with learning problems accompanied by a physical defect. He could not read at all. The eye clinic informed us that he was almost blind in one eye. He never wore his glasses. After many weeks of discussion he was persuaded to bring them and to wear them for at least ten minutes. By the end of that time he was almost in tears. He could hardly draw, and he was good at drawing. He could not read one word. It seemed that the glasses were meant to exercise his good eye. They would probably have been beneficial over time, but there was no encouragement at home and he rarely brought his glasses to school. Adrian learned to read in spite of his physical defect. He was one of those children who became very anti-social as he began to learn. There were many problems in his home background. When he was 12 he was transferred to a day school for maladjusted children where he became a 'star pupil'. Again, it is difficult to know to what extent his physical defect contributed to his learning and behaviour problems.

Other sensory deficits that are very difficult to establish are intermittent deafness and intermittent squint. The terms are self-explanatory. The child is sometimes deaf and sometimes hears quite well. Similarly, he squints at times and sees normally at others. Naturally his learning will be affected. He is also likely to worry about it, but as he will not know that he is different from other children he will not be able to talk about his anxieties.

Specific spelling difficulties

Specific learning difficulties appear also in spelling and arithmetic. Some aspects of specific spelling difficulties and their remediation are very lucidly discussed by Peters (1970). Spelling is, of course, very closely related to reading and it can be expected that children with reading difficulties will have similar difficulties in spelling. There are also a number of children who can read fluently, but whose spelling is very incorrect and very erratic and who do not seem to be able to improve by practice. This kind of spelling disability is not infrequent with very intelligent children.

In my experience specific spelling disability can be extremely difficult to remedy. The treatment of Ronald suggests some of the underlying problems. Ronald was referred by his school at the age of 15. He was bright and passed GCE 'O' level in several subjects, but he made at least one spelling mistake in every line he wrote. It was often quite impossible to understand what he wanted to say. By the time he left school at 16, he had learned a number of spelling rules and he was able to recognise whether or not he had spelled a word correctly. With the help of a dictionary he could therefore produce a perfect piece of writing. Two years afterwards he approached us again for help. He was now an apprentice in electrical design and his employer had advised him to seek help with his spelling. In the course of the next two years it became evident to what extent his disability was connected with his home background, particularly with his relationship with his father. His father was a self-made man, who expected his son to make good use of the education that the father had never been able to obtain. The son's bad spelling was his way of rebelling against his father's pressures while remaining the polite, amenable boy that he was. There were many other factors that could have contributed to the spelling difficulty. He was also rather a lonely young man. He had very few friends. The interesting aspect of Ronald's treatment was that direct teaching did not help him in any appreciable way. At one stage he told me that on attempting to spell a word he had before his eyes a big black cloud with some letters emerging and that he had to reconstruct each word from its aural aspect. In consequence, he often chose the wrong letter combination for a particular word, e.g. writing 'maine' when he intended to write 'main'. There

69

was, however, a considerable improvement when his attitude towards his father began to change. He still made
mistakes, but one could understand what he wanted to
communicate and he was able to pass the national certifi-
cate of proficiency for which he was studying.

Difficulties with arithmetic

Difficulty with number is, I think, quite different. Some
children have a problem about accuracy that is very annoying to them and to their teacher, but these careless mistakes
will not prevent them from learning mathematical principles. Other children have difficulty with specific processes, such as division or subtraction, often because they
were away or inattentive when this process was introduced
and later did not ask for clarification for fear of arousing
the teacher's anger with so stupid a question. These problems can generally be alleviated in a comparatively short
time if the child is given systematic help.

There are, however, some children who have difficulties
with the simplest processes such as counting or simple
addition. These children are generally very disturbed or
have had quite serious illnesses such as meningitis or con-
vulsions in their early infancy. The arithmetic disability
is rarely their only handicap. They are often in schools for
educationally subnormal children, because their overall
intellectual functioning is affected as well. These children
are generally only able to learn with concrete apparatus,
such as counters, and are unable to do even the simplest
sum in their heads.

Martin, for instance, had an organic condition, i.e. he
had a lesion in some part of his brain. He could not count
at all at the age of 10. After receiving help for nine months
he was able to count up to 100 with counters, he could
add hundreds and tens and units with the help of a special
piece of apparatus. He had even begun to do some simple
multiplication with counters, but he could not add or

subtract 1 in his head. On the other hand he had learned to read and was able to read books for pleasure.

I have described these specific learning disabilities in such detail because they cause many teachers and parents a great deal of concern. All teachers have very mixed feelings when their pupils do not progress, particularly when they fail to learn, but appear bright and interested outside the lessons. Many teachers blame themselves for the child's lack of progress. Others blame the child. This discussion is an attempt to increase the understanding of why a particular child might not be able to learn.

Children with low general ability

Finally, I should like to consider those children whose overall intellectual functioning is affected. It is well known that these children are incapable of learning as effectively and quickly as ordinary children. Again, it is important that the teacher spots them as early as possible. Yet, again, it is not always easy to distinguish them from those children who have specific learning difficulties and who are anti-social, apathetic or immature. Ideally, they should be referred for assessment as soon as the school feels that there might be a possibility of intellectual impairment. They can be relatively easily and reliably assessed by an educational psychologist. However, there is a stigma attached to special education and if the child is well behaved and friendly the teachers are inclined to keep him on. Many primary school teachers are also very skilful in helping a slow learning child, even in a group of more intelligent children.

It is difficult to judge what is best for such children. Some of them can proceed from primary school to secondary school and do quite well in spite of their handicap. Others fail at the secondary school stage when failure is more difficult to bear than when they are younger. Again, each child will benefit most if he can be considered in his own right. Until recently the regulations for placement into schools for educationally subnormal children, as they are called, were very rigid. A child 'qualified' if his IQ was 80 or lower. In recent years the rules have become a little more flexible, and this should profit many children in the long run.

Remediation of learning difficulties

Learning difficulties therefore, like behaviour problems, are difficult to diagnose. They are often accompanied by other difficulties. They are caused by a variety of factors and they worry the teachers. Some of these conditions can be remedied by the class teacher himself, some need special arrangements in school, such as a remedial class. Some need treatment in a different institution such as an ESN school or a Child Guidance Clinic. The more observant, the more open-minded a teacher can be, the more effective he will be in finding the help these children need.

7
The withdrawn, inattentive child

The inattentive, docile, withdrawn child usually only begins to worry a teacher when he is identified as having a learning problem. I have already mentioned that in the sample of 51 children, who were treated for severe reading disability, 17 fell into this group. Some of these have already been described. Arnold, for instance, just sat at the back of the class and did nothing. Adrian was also very passive before he began to learn. Neither Arnold nor Adrian would have caused concern to their teachers if it had not been for their learning problem. Yet their subsequent aggressive behaviour showed them to be severely emotionally disturbed.

There is, to my mind, a very good reason why these children are so often missed. If one thinks of the difficulty involved in dealing with a class in terms of a large group, the teacher is likely to be quite relieved to find some children docile and amenable, and if their attainment seems to be within the range of their ability, the teacher will not think that there might be anything wrong. Besides, it is very difficult to define the withdrawn child. Where is the borderline between over-docility and obedience? How can you ascertain that the quiet boy at the back of the class is, in fact, inattentive, as long as his work is done more or less all right? His reticence might just be shyness.

An underfunctioning grammar school child

This is a particularly important problem when a child is intelligent enough to be able to do adequate work and appears to work to the best of his ability. Such a child may be much more intelligent than he appears to be, and may have learning difficulties as severe and disabling as the child who is retarded in reading or spelling. Alice was a case in point. She shared characteristics very similar to those of Arnold and Adrian. She was a quiet, apparently rather dull girl of 12 in a grammar school. She was also very fat. She never expressed an opinion about anything and she never told anybody what she felt.

I was Alice's form-mistress at that time. I also taught her Latin. She was conscientious, but not very good at it. She always did what was asked of her. I knew that she was not very popular, but her class-mates were not unfriendly either.

I always had kept a little money in the teacher's desk. Sometimes I needed some change when I collected the dinner money. Over some period of time I thought that some of this money was missing. It was so little that I did not take much notice of it. Yet sometimes I wondered whether somebody was taking it and who it might be.

One day, Alice's class saw a film in another classroom together with another class. One of the girls had left some money in her desk and after the film half of the money was missing. Fortunately, I could remember that Alice had sat in this seat. I challenged her and she returned the money. She also told me that she had taken small amounts of money from the cloakrooms and from my desk.

Very shortly afterwards Alice was given a group intelligence test together with all the children of her year. To the great surprise of her teachers this girl, who was considered dull by everyone, passed in the top division. The teachers argued that the tests were faulty. They never considered the stealing incident as a means of drawing attention to her under-functioning. In this way, this potentially clever girl never worked on a level comparable to her intelligence. She continued to be rather lonely and unhappy. It seemed that her parents, too, were accepting the rather low standard of her work and did not query why she did not do better when she had been able to pass the 11-plus examination. Neither they nor the school medical officer took the stealing incident for what I think it was—a cry for help. An attempt to obtain psychiatric treatment for Alice failed.

Eddy, the slightly odd boy

Another category of quiet, withdrawn children is characterised by slightly odd behaviour that can be easily missed. Eddy, for instance, was thought to be peculiar because of his very odd and confused stories. He was in a junior school and 10 years old. He had few friends and a very difficult home background. His stories were like dreams, without any logic. He found it difficult to distinguish between his dreams and reality. Eddy was a scruffy little boy with rather ineffective parents. The teachers did not query his odd stories, but his headmistress was concerned and Eddy was put into a special class and profited a great deal from the help he received there.

Referrals of withdrawn children are very often initiated by their parents, who are not content with their child's work, very much to the surprise of their teachers.

The problems of a very bright child

Michael, aged 11, for instance, was referred for investigation privately. He went to a very well-known grammar school and was just able to follow the course. His teachers thought him to be just one of those children whose work deteriorates when it becomes more difficult. He had obviously been very good in his primary school but, of course, he did not have as much competition there.

His parents, however, were puzzled and not content with the teacher's explanation. On testing, Michael was found to be of exceptionally high intelligence, but he failed on some of the easy items. His performance improved as the subtests became more difficult. His trouble was partly that he was bored. The progress in class was too slow for him. But he had also found the transfer from the small intimate primary school to the large grammar school very difficult and, being the only one of his area who passed the entrance examination to this school, he had to leave all his friends behind. With very little help Michael's school work improved, but one wonders what would have happened if his parents had not been so observant.

Intelligent children who do not reach their potential are probably much more frequent than any of us realise. Of course, none of us really do, as Vernon (1969) points out. Moreover, it is usually very difficult to help children whose intellectual functioning is affected by emotional disturbance, particularly if this is linked to early experiences. However, there are a number of children on all intelligence levels whose problems are more like those of Michael and who can be helped quite easily. The National Association for Gifted Children is to some extent looking after those who are very bright, if they are detected by teachers or parents. As teachers we can only be on the look-out for these children so that we can help them. With behaviour problems and severe learning problems being on the increase, it is likely that these children may continue to be neglected.

8
The school refuser

This chapter and the next will deal with a different kind of disturbance, in as far as the children are not only behaving in an undesirable way at school, but their behaviour is also punishable by law. Some time ago I talked about school refusers to a group of teachers. Amongst them was a teacher from the Cameroons. He declared that this problem was unknown in his country. In his country it is such a privilege to have a place in a school that a child who did not want to attend was at once replaced by another. So the parents saw to it that their child would not jeopardise his privileged position.

School refusal and the law

School refusal differs from the other difficulties discussed in another way: there can be no doubt in the teacher's mind that a child who is absent from school without a valid reason is a school refuser. They are easy to spot. Besides, the school refuser is not troublesome *in* class, he is worrying the teacher because he is *out of* class.

Naturally, teachers are afraid that the school refuser is staying away because he does not like their teaching. To some degree this is justified, not very often because of the inadequacy of an individual teacher, much more frequently because of special demands made by our school system. For instance, it is well known that school refusal increases considerably at transfer from primary to secondary school.

Transfer from primary to secondary school

Adrian, whom I have quoted previously, was a case in point. His primary school had been round the corner from his home. He had known his headmistress and many of the teachers for many years. So had the parents. He had stayed away from school now and then, but when that had happened, the headmistress had sent one of the helpers around to his home to find out why he had not come. Sometimes his mother was ill and he had to look after his younger brothers and sisters, sometimes he just had not felt like going to school. The helper had then taken him by the hand and they had gone to school together or, if he was needed at home, the helper informed the headmistress who then excused his absence.

In his new comprehensive school Adrian seemed bewildered. He hardly knew any of the teachers. He often did not appear in a lesson because he did not know what room to go to at any particular time. In break time he was often reprimanded by a stranger, an unknown teacher or a prefect with whom he had no relationship at all. Adrian did not talk about this, he just stayed away and said he did not like school. His mother was very worried about this and when I saw them about it, his mother reminded him that he liked at least one lesson each day and was able to persuade him to have another try. In time, he adjusted to the size and the life of the large school. He also became very fond of the remedial teacher who took his class for most lessons. The reader will remember that, when his teacher left, he became so unmanageable that the school could contain him no longer and he was transferred to a day school for maladjusted children. In his case this was a blessing in disguise. In the setting of this special school he was able to obtain the help that nobody else could have given him.

Truancy

Many pupils of secondary schools stay away and spend the day elsewhere, often in the company of their friends and without the knowledge of their parents. This problem of truancy is presently increasing on a grand scale. It is not particularly helped by the necessity for part-time education caused by staff shortage in many schools. Teachers' strikes may also contribute. Many of the children we have in treatment expressed great concern about it. Most of them come from unstable homes. It seemed as if the one pillar of stability in their lives had crumbled. This does not necessarily mean that teachers should not take industrial action. It only points to one of the problems that occurs if they do. It is also obvious that children will find it easier to 'walk out' if teachers do.

In my opinion the teacher shortages and walk-outs are only of very minor importance. Nor do I think that the increase of difficult children is the main reason for this massive truancy. I think that most of these children do not attend because they cannot see what profit they will derive from sitting through their lessons. They find them boring, they make no progress and they are not likely to succeed in examinations. So why go?

In the literature, truancy, as this kind of behaviour is often called, is often contrasted with 'school phobia'. The difference is often difficult to ascertain. In general, school phobia is accompanied by signs of anxiety in connection with school attendance. The child often shows physical symptoms like vomiting or headaches in the morning, or very obvious signs of anxiety before entering school, such as trembling. These children usually overtly express a wish to go to school and seem to be quite happy and content in school if they can get themselves there. Their parents are usually very much aware of their children's problems. There are a great many reasons for this kind of behaviour, very ably described by Kahn and Nursten (1964). These children are often more concerned with staying at home rather than going to school. Sometimes their parents, particularly their mother, unconsciously wish them to stay, although they are consciously very concerned about the child's non-attendance.

School refusal and the family

Such a tie existed between 10-year-old Clare and her mother. There was a rather passive father who was not able to take any leadership in the family. Although every member of the family was anxious that Clare should go to school, each one also had unconscious reasons that made this impossible. Clare hardly ever went away from home. She did not want to go anywhere. She could not give reasons for it, but it emerged that she could not leave her mother who was physically ill, because she feared her mother would die while she was away. Clare was unaware of these and a number of other feelings which caused this intense anxiety.

Michael, aged 6, and his parents also had a lot of problems. Michael had never been away from school, but every morning there were tears when his mother was taking him to school. After some psychiatric treatment of the family it became clear that to some degree father expected Michael to do badly at school, because of his own experiences at school. Father thought of himself as a failure in school, because he felt that his own parents expected him to be like his brilliant brother. He did not want Michael to do any better than himself. Michael never actually became a school refuser, mainly because his very observant teachers had referred him so early. His problems were, in fact, very complex. From an unhappy, quiet little boy he changed into a child with behaviour problems, with a particular difficulty in sharing the teacher, often expressed by attacking other children viciously. These problems emerged when the issue of school attendance had cleared up.

Stanley

Stanley (see Caspari and Osborne,1967), another secondary school boy, had other kinds of problems connected with school attendance. His older brother had died before he was born and this had led to his parents' rather over-protective attitude towards him, and an extremely close relationship between him and his mother to the exclusion of anybody else in the family. The elder brother had died in an accident so it was not surprising that Stanley's parents were over-protective. Long before Stanley had begun to stay away from school he had been known to be very quiet and shy. He seldom played with children of his own age, preferring to play with much younger children. The parents reported that he had temper tantrums and screaming fits at home, usually when his three sisters teased him. They often called him a 'mummy's boy' and seemed to be jealous of him.

Stanley started to truant when he was about 13 years old. He had never been in any trouble at school and was doing quite well. The parents did not know about the truancy until they were informed of his non-attendance by the Educational Welfare Officer. Mother kept this information away from father at first, but when the headmaster asked the parents to come and see him father also found out that Stanley had truanted.

Stanley had stayed away from school not because he did not like it but because he had found it unbearable to be in the classroom together with children of his own age. The teacher reported that he grew pale and showed signs of great anxiety when he was asked to join his age group. Why this difficulty had come up at that particular time

81

never became apparent. It is possible that it had something to do with adolescence, a time when problems become intensified.

Stanley was helped by the school and the clinic. The school made arrangements for him to work in the library or at the back of another class, and under these conditions he attended regularly. The clinic tried to help him and his parents to come to terms with some of the problems that had led to his school refusal. At one time the school had to put pressure on the family, for the parents wanted to discontinue their meetings at the clinic, thinking that this was not necessary now that Stanley attended school regularly again. The headmaster saw the family at that point and explained to them that Stanley's regular attendance was closely linked to the special arrangements that the school had made for him. These caused a great deal of extra work for his teachers who had to set him special work and correct it. The headmaster made it clear that the school could not go on with these arrangements indefinitely. Other children in the school also began to feel that Stanley was favoured. The teachers thought that Stanley was not yet able to return to his class and the headmaster predicted that the truanting would start again if Stanley was asked to join his own class. So the family continued to attend the clinic until the end of the school year. After the summer holidays Stanley returned to his class.

To some degree Stanley's attachment to his mother was very similar to the tie between Clare and her mother. In both families there was a rather weak, condoning father. Yet the strength of the ties within the two families were different, and Stanley's parents could more easily accept that their fear for Stanley's safety was not really justified. So Stanley could be helped far more quickly than Clare.

Dorian

In both these cases some of the reasons for the school

refusal could be detected and discussed. This is not always so. Dorian, for instance, had stayed away for several weeks and his parents had told the headmaster of his secondary school that they were worried about it. Dorian was in his second year at school. When he first came he had refused to go to games. The school had no playing fields and the children were taken to a sportsground by bus. The teachers had made allowances for his dislike of games and he was permitted to stay at school during this time. Towards the end of the year he had also refused to take part in PE lessons, and after that he stayed away altogether.

The headmaster and I saw the parents together to see what could be done. During the interview all sorts of problems were discussed. The parents reported that Dorian had nightmares and suffered from sleepwalking. His mother also walked in her sleep. There were several other problems, none of them obviously related to his staying away from school, and we discussed these with the parents, mainly to explore whether the parents would accept help from the clinic. They did not and I never heard from them again. However, after this episode Dorian attended school regularly. Neither the headmaster nor I could account for this, but the headmaster was very pleased. Whether Dorian could have been helped with his many deep-seated problems if the urgency of help had continued, one does not, of course, know.

We often feel something must be wrong when problems like school refusal suddenly occur. Yet often we ought to be glad about it as the case of Adrian has shown. It is frequently a cry for help, the child is saying, 'There is something wrong with me, take notice', and doing something that is ultimately punishable by law is the surest way of being noticed. Maybe the interview with Dorian's parents helped them to realise that Dorian's nightmares and sleepwalking indicated that he was unhappy and worried so that he no longer needed to stay away from school in order to draw attention to his unhappiness. Maybe, once Dorian had experienced that his parents were worried about him and cared, he no longer had a need to cause them concern in this way.

None of the children quoted actually got into trouble with the law. There are several reasons for this. When a child stays away from school, the parents will be informed and will be told that they will be prosecuted if they do not take steps to see that their child goes to school. If they seek help from a Child Guidance Clinic and are found to have problems, such as the ones we have seen, the workers of the Child Guidance Clinic will contact the authorities, usually the Educational Welfare Officer, and will discuss with them what plans can be made. Clare, for instance, had home tuition for a time by a teacher employed by the LEA to help children who for one reason or another cannot go to school. Stanley's teachers, as we have seen, made special arrangements for him.

Sam

Sam's case shows a different variation of the theme of school refusal. There was also a special tie between him and his mother, but in his case it was linked to his parents' divorce. Sam was 13 and the eldest boy in the family. When he began to stay away from school, his mother had just come out of mental hospital. He and his younger brother had stayed with his maternal grandparents. The three remaining siblings had been in care. He was referred to the clinic by a social worker who was supporting his mother. He had only been away from school for a fortnight when he was referred. He was very depressed about the divorce. He was very anxious that something might happen to his mother. He was able to speak quite freely about his problems and about his unhappiness, and he was able to say that he did not really know why he did not want to go to school. We tried to help this family by discussing their problems with them, but in this case we were

84

entirely unsuccessful. On the contrary, Sam's younger brother, Michael, also began to stay away. Mother's boy-friend might have aggravated the problem. He had a great grudge against authority in general, and schools and mental health institutions in particular, and actively encouraged the boys to stay away. After a year the boys were placed in a day hostel for maladjusted children.

How the school can help

I hope that these examples demonstrate that school refusal is generally a sign of considerable disturbance in a child and his family and that the problems need not necessarily have much to do with his going to school.

In spite of this, teachers can often do a great deal to alleviate the underlying unhappiness by their attempt to understand the child's behaviour, as well as by adapting the school's pattern to the child's needs. These may include the need for punishment. Teachers are, of course, not always successful, nor are any of us, but we can try.

9
The delinquent

Delinquency has many facets and is as difficult to define as any of the other patterns of behaviour that characterise difficult children. Like the school refuser, the delinquent can be punished by law, so the delinquent act is often as much a cry for help as school refusal. Like school refusal, delinquency can appear suddenly and disappear again; it can also go on for years and years.

The problem of delinquency is discussed in great detail in the Isle of Wight study (Rutter, 1970) under the main heading of anti-social disorders, subdivided according to the extent of delinquency. Special attention is also given to what is phrased 'socialised delinquency', a term used to characterise those children whose delinquent acts are directed against society as a whole, but are accepted by the sub-culture to which the child belongs, his delinquent family for instance, or a delinquent gang.

Delinquency and learning problems—Kay

Many delinquent children are also very naughty in class, and have often been so long before they committed a delinquent act. Some of them have also severe learning disabilities. There is a great deal of debate as to which is the chicken and which is the egg. Do the children become delinquent because they are frustrated in school, or do they become backward because the conflicts that cause the delinquency prevent them from concentrating on their work?

Experience leads me to believe that in many cases these two aspects of behaviour are different reactions to very similar problems. All these children are unhappy and angry and have severe difficulties in finding ways of expressing their anger in a socially acceptable way. Those that are naughty and/or delinquent show their anger by attacking society, those that just cannot learn prevent their anger from being expressed by being passive and uncommunicative. Some, as we have seen, change from one group to the other. When Adrian was just sitting in class and not learning, he did not express any feelings at all. When he began to learn he began to show his feelings of anger, and then could only express them in an anti-social, delinquent way.

Kay, aged 12, gives a much clearer picture of the link between learning disability and delinquency, mainly because we were able to find out much more about his home circumstances.

Kay was almost a non-reader when he was referred. His teachers reported that he was a pleasant, quiet lad, who did not do any work at all, but who did not cause any trouble either. Little was known about his family. Kay had told one of the teachers that he had lived in Ireland with his grandmother and that his grandmother had died some time ago. Kay was illegitimate and it seemed that he had had little attention from his mother. Since his grandmother's death he was living with his mother. It was known to the school that mother was living with another man. Just before Kay was given special help with his reading, his mother had let it be known that she had married.

Kay profited greatly from his treatment and his reading improved very quickly. So did his school work as a whole. At the same time he began to be associated with two rather anti-social boys in his class. He began to imitate their aggressive behaviour and the teachers began to complain about him. Shortly afterwards he was taken to court for what was officially called 'robbery with violence'. It emerged that Kay and his two friends had seen an old lady with a bag and had decided to take the bag away from her. Whose idea it had originally been was not clear, Kay took action while the other two looked on. The old lady held on to her bag and in an attempt to take it by force, Kay pulled the old lady down. He was given a probation order.

Kay's story is a very good example of a delinquent act as a cry for help. For when the probation officer began to investigate he found that Kay and his mother lived in one room and shared the same bed. At this time Kay was nearly 13. Kay's stepfather worked away from home but returned now and then, and where Kay slept when stepfather was at home nobody ever found out. It also emerged that mother suffered from epileptic fits and Kay had to look after her and himself on these occasions. The probation service helped in two ways: they supported Kay and his mother by discussing their problems with them, but they also saw to it that the family was rehoused so that Kay got a room of his own.

Kay's behaviour improved and so did his reading. He never committed a delinquent act again. Unfortunately, however, his educational therapist left and he did not want to start with a stranger. His reading had improved sufficiently for him to hold his own in the class and he liked his probation officer and saw him regularly.

A year later I made enquiries about him at school. There were no complaints, but he had reverted to his quiet, withdrawn behaviour and did very little work. His teacher did not think that Kay was unduly worried by his lack of progress. He was able to hold his own in the remedial class and got on reasonably well with his teachers and his peers. It was difficult to see what help a Child Guidance Clinic could offer him now. He had never been very articulate and we felt that an hour a week to talk about his problems would not be of much help. Like many delinquents he would have needed an opportunity to express his angry feelings in action, like Dick in the school for maladjusted children, but this would not have been appropriate for Kay, who had no behaviour problem.

Delinquency and inability to make close relationships— John

John was another type of delinquent. He belonged to the group whose main difficulties lie in their inability to make close relationships and in experiencing feelings of guilt. It is extremely difficult to spot these children, because they might be very charming on first acquaintance. He was another adolescent, 14 years old. He was discussed by a group of teachers, just after he had been to court because he had broken into a house with a friend and had ransacked all the Christmas cards in search of money. Each teacher reported in turn how difficult he was, how he interfered with their lessons, how he quarrelled with other boys. He had attacked one boy with a test tube, he did not do any work, he was insolent to the teachers and he generally got under everybody's skin. Only one teacher disagreed: with him John was pleasant, charming, very willing to help, no trouble at all. This teacher was new and had only known John for a few weeks. His colleagues told him that they had experienced similar behaviour from John when they first met him. The new teacher was adamant in his claim that only he was able to deal with John, although he was, of course, too polite to say so openly. A few months later John committed another offence and was placed in an approved school.

The underlying causes for John's behaviour were only partly known. His parents were divorced, and his mother blamed the school for John's bad behaviour. John's behaviour, however, seemed to show that he tried to make a good, close relationship with every new adult he met, but after a while he became disillusioned. The adult did not come up to John's expectations, so John was disappointed and angry and showed his anger by anti-social behaviour.

Like many other delinquents John wanted money and set about getting it in rather unreasonable ways. Money is seldom enclosed in Christmas cards. He also entered the house in such an obvious way that he had to be found out and caught. It almost seemed as if he wanted to be caught, like many other delinquents, juvenile and adult. It seemed as if he wanted to demonstrate that he was neglected—the Christmas cards were sent to somebody else and not to him. This demonstration would not have served any purpose if he had not been found out—so he arranged the theft in such a way that he had to be caught.

The underlying causes for this type of behaviour can usually be found in the very early life of these children. Bowlby (1946) suggested that they are linked to what is often called 'maternal deprivation'. This term suggests that these people have been neglected by their mothers in early infancy. To some degree this is true, but it is very difficult to describe this neglect. It very rarely means that the mother did not care. It often can be seen that the mother could not look after her baby because of illness, death or other reasons beyond her control. Often a neglected child finds someone else, a mother substitute, and will grow up into an ordinary healthy child. The trouble is that the underlying reasons are so difficult to discover. The children cannot remember their infancy and the memory of the adults is often blurred. The worst part of the problem is that we are still very unclear as to ways and means of helping these children.

Problems of helping delinquents

They can be helped most effectively the way Dick was helped: by showing a person they like their worst behaviour and by experiencing that this person can accept them in spite of it. Only this experience can convince a child that he is lovable and acceptable, and only if he feels himself valued can he, himself, adjust to the demands of society.

Some institutions can provide this experience, but there are not many of them. There are not many people who can go through with a treatment of this kind. It is difficult to describe what demands for tolerance these children make on such people. It is, indeed, remarkable that these people can carry it through. Fortunately, they do and perhaps we will learn to value their services more than we presently do, and we will organise this kind of work in a more realistic way. Experience has shown that punishment and detention in community centres and borstals do not work. Detention of juveniles in borstals has been discontinued. The probation service is to be extended to deal with juvenile delinquents. Probation officers themselves are doubtful whether they are able to help these children effectively. I am inclined to agree, but I do think that this change is the first step towards finding a more adequate way of helping this group of children.

Part Three

The teacher as helping agent to troublesome children

10
Class management and teaching techniques

At this stage some readers might feel discouraged and despondent. How is one to assure class control when the classroom situation itself leads to troublesome behaviour and when it is unavoidable that some children in one's class have problems of their own and will be very difficult to contain.

To make matters worse, there are indications that the percentage of emotionally disturbed children is increasing.

The remedies commonly advocated are twofold: there is constant political pressure to reduce the size of classes and there is a tendency to segregate the difficult children in special schools and classes.

In practice, however, these remedies have only worked within limits. Economic considerations have kept the classes large except perhaps for some reductions in primary schools. Similarly, the special schools and classes are so overcrowded that it often takes 6-12 months to obtain a place for a child even in those areas with comparatively generous provision.

In my opinion, there is a need for smaller classes and there is a need for special education for special children. But there is also a need to examine what contributions the organisation of the school and the teacher's skill can make to the solution of this problem.

Often teachers will attribute their ability to maintain class control to certain mannerisms, such as speaking in a quiet voice, or to organisational factors, such as insisting that the children put their pencils on the desk when they are listening to instruction, or that they stand quietly in line before leaving the classroom. No doubt, these factors contribute to the smooth and happy interrelationship between them and their pupils, but if another teacher adopts their 'methods' he often finds them completely ineffective.

Considering the complexity of the situation that we discussed it is not very surprising that such 'gimmicks' do not work. If we consider that the way a teacher acts will be influenced not only by his thoughts, ideals and principles, but also by his conscious and unconscious feelings and his skill in reacting to the feelings of his pupils, it becomes obvious that there is no simple solution. Some people might feel that it is all a matter of personality and that it is futile to look for principles. This is, of course, true up to a point. It is true of all professions. Yet if one supports the view that 'teachers' are 'born' and not 'made' to the exclusion of everything else, one might well give up training them.

I should therefore like to examine some of the factors that were found to contribute to troublesome behaviour in class and consider to what extent attention given to these factors might make the situation more manageable.

The importance of meaningful activities

Let us start with the concept of a class as a large group. It was mentioned earlier that large groups appear to be very dependent on their leaders. It therefore stands to reason that class control could be facilitated if the leader, the teacher, is accepted by members of the group. It has, of course, always been recognised that 'children will behave themselves' if they like their teacher. However, this has often been understood in terms of liking the teacher as a person. This is, of course, important, but in my opinion the management of the class depends first and foremost on whether or not the teacher has caught the pupils' interest and attention. Hourd (1972) has written about this in great detail and with great insight. One of her most striking passages is the one in which she refers to *The Tempest* and suggests that 'in one aspect of his personality Prospero is the arch-teacher' who worked on a magic island with Ariel, 'the embodiment of the power and suggestion'. She explores this theme at some length, stressing among other things, the magic that makes the lesson a very special experience. However, the magic can only work if it is felt not only by the children, but by the teacher, too. Unfortunately, this is not always so.

Some years ago I was leading some seminar groups of very experienced teachers within the framework of an advanced training course on the topic of supervision of teaching practice. One of these teachers gave an account of a student's lesson in nature study. The topic was seed dispersal. The student had experienced a considerable amount of disciplinary difficulties during this lesson and the discussion explored many of the contributory factors which, to me, though relevant, seemed to be off-centre. In the end I could not contain myself any longer and suggested that, to my mind, the lesson had been incredibly dull. A number of the group members agreed, but others went to the student's defence. The lesson was no duller than many others they had seen, they said, and anyhow, the topic was dull, so how could the student give an interesting lesson? Moreover, the topic was not of her choice. The class teacher had requested it.

The teacher and the demands of the curriculum

To some extent I was saddened by these remarks. To me the process of seed dispersal is of intense interest and excitement, but I could see that it might not appeal to everyone. I was also perturbed by the suggestion that so much of our teaching is expected to be dull.

On the other hand, what was the relevance of seed

dispersal to these particular children? By what right do we teach these children what we do teach them at the time we teach it? For example, why should anybody but a classical scholar learn Latin in this day and age? Why should junior school children be taught long division when this process can easily be performed by a simple and not very expensive computer? Why should an 'A' level course in foreign languages be restricted to the study of certain set books? Have we not, all of us, taken lessons on topics that were not of intrinsic interest to us?

Indeed, these are problems which will always be with every teacher. Whatever he teaches will, to some degree, be determined by the curriculum, and he cannot expect the whole curriculum to be entirely to his liking. Naturally, the curriculum might leave more or less flexibility to the teacher. In our educational system, for instance, the curriculum in primary schools is more flexible than that of secondary schools, and this may be one of the many reasons that make class control in secondary schools more difficult at present. Be that as it may: the basic question is, in my opinion, whether or not the external obligations are so contrary to our interests that we cannot find anything valuable in the subject matter at all, or whether it is possible to adapt the external pressures to our own preferences.

If the answer is that we cannot see any value at all, I do not think that we can continue with our work. If we do not feel that what we present to our pupils is of value to them, we have no chance to interest them and we can only maintain control by coercion and force. Most of the time, however, it is, I think, possible to find some aspects of the curriculum that may be of value and to arrange the lesson so that the pupils can get something out of it.

To give an example: during my teaching career in a grammar school I was asked to take beginners' Latin with a group of 12-year-olds who were expected to give it up after two years. I felt very unenthusiastic about this assignment. Although I had studied Latin myself up to 'A' level, I had never felt very enthusiastic about it. I liked some of the literature, but that was irrelevant to the task. The curriculum did not include literature. I was interested in Roman history and in my study of modern languages I had found my knowledge of Latin useful in connection with derivation of words and the history of languages. I disliked the very complicated grammar and the attention to detail one had to give to every word, and I realised that my task was most closely connected with that aspect of Latin. I was also aware that, whatever I did, the children would connect their learning of Latin with failure. They knew that they would give it up and that they had not been considered 'clever enough' to be allocated to the group which was expected to continue. Like many teachers I did not have a choice to refuse. It was part of the contract and I was interested in the other work I did at the school.

So I had to make what I could of the job. In the end I concentrated on two aspects: first, on the satisfaction the pupils might get from success, and second, on the opportunity they might have to make English grammar more meaningful to them. I do not consider the study of English grammar of intrinsic interest to children of 11 and 12 either, but at least I knew that the majority of pupils take 'O' level examinations in English language, so this aspect of my Latin lessons would, at least, not be completely wasted. The satisfaction through success was more fundamental, as it counterbalanced the sense of failure derived from being members of a group which was not expected to continue.

Learning plateaux and the importance of success

Moreover, success can be seen as one of the most satisfying aspects of learning in general because it demonstrates, in a tangible way, the individual's mastery over the environ-

99

ment. Very often learning is so frustrating because one cannot see one's success. This is particularly true of the learning of skills, when one arrives at a so-called 'learning plateau', the stage of acquiring a skill, when one thinks one can drive a car, yet fails the driving test because one has not been able to master all of it, or when one does not seem to make any tangible progress in the learning of a foreign language. Therefore, a logical subject, such as fundamental aspects of Latin grammar, lends itself superbly to give tangible evidence for success.

So I decided that it was immaterial how much Latin these children would learn, as long as they could experience success in the tasks I asked them to do. I actually introduced the study of Latin as a kind of puzzle. I think the teacher in charge of Latin in the school would have raised her hands in horror if she had known; but it worked. The girls worked well. There is an ironic twist to this story: just before I left teaching, there was a general inspection of the school and I was told that the inspector was particularly impressed by my Latin lessons!

I realise that what I am saying might be controversial. Many educationalists think the other way round. They buy a machine and arrange the presentation around the particular programme the machine facilitates. Their love of the machine and the power of suggestion that goes with it very often assures their success. There is nothing wrong with this, except that one needs to realise that another teacher who does not like the machine all that much, or who is not so enthusiastic about the particular programme, is not likely to succeed to the same degree.

Prescribed programmes: teaching to read as an illustration of their uses and limitations

This dilemma can be vividly illustrated in the field of teaching to read. There is an extensive literature about methods of learning to read, from Monroe (1932) to Downing (1964), illustrating the success of the method discussed. Considering the great controversies in this field, e.g. that between learning by phonic method or learning by whole word method, this seems surprising. There are only few instances when methods have been followed up (e.g. Downing, 1967) and these follow-up studies have generally shown some limitations of the initial success. In most cases teachers have just stopped using the particular method or they have adapted it to the needs of their pupils.

Personally, I am grateful to anyone who invents a new method because it enriches the opportunities for learning. This is essential when one deals with children who cannot learn. In my own work with children with severe reading disability I cannot follow any one method rigidly. Let us assume I find that the pupil cannot read one single word and is quite unaware of the significance of sounds in reading. It would be useless to attempt phonics at this stage so I decide that the child needs a whole-word approach. I then look around for books or apparatus. I could use the *Breakthrough to Literacy* (1970), or a reading series like the Macmillan Readers (1950), or simply use the child's own headings for his own pictures to build up his vocabulary. My decision will depend on my judgment of the speed with which he would learn, and my method of approach would be constantly modified by my observations of his behaviour. At one stage I would probably find that his memory for words is too unreliable for him to remember more than a limited number of words. I would probably also have observed that he is beginning to understand the use of letter sounds. He might use initial sounds for guessing words he cannot read immediately. We might have played a game of 'I spy', and he might have shown his knowledge of sounds to me in that way. I might then decide that the child now needs a phonic approach because this will diminish the number of words he has to remember. He could use the phonics as props when his memory would let him down. I can then examine the vast number of phonic apparatus, Stott's Programmed Reading Kit (1962), Moxon's Remedial Reading Method (1962), or the talking typewriter, and might decide then what to use, again modifying my approach according to the child's rate of progress.

I think most remedial teachers work in a similar way when they teach a child individually. I should like to suggest that there is no difference in principle when one teaches a large group. It is more difficult and other factors such as organisation or different rates of learning need to be taken into account. It is also more difficult to get feedback from the children because one cannot observe them so closely. But the principle still holds.

The interesting lesson as the basis for class control

This discussion has been rather rambling, but for an important reason : in considering how to obtain class control, the children's interest in the lesson is to my mind the central factor. If the children are not interested there is bound to be trouble, unless the teacher is so authoritarian that the children obey out of fear. They usually compensate for this by being unruly with another teacher who is less austere.

To make lessons interesting is not, to my mind, easy, but it is absolutely essential. Naturally, day in, day out, not every lesson can be exciting, but at least the pupil needs to know the purpose of the activity. None of us adults would willingly attend a course at a university or a similar institution, unless we find the experience valuable. If we do not, we refuse to attend. Unfortunately, we often follow a boring course in spite of our dislike of it because of the value of the qualifications we obtain at the end of the course.

This is perhaps one of the reasons why the presentation of the subject matter does not receive as much attention as it might, particularly in secondary schools. Pupils in

secondary schools are expected to work for their qualifications, for their 'A' levels, their 'O' levels or their CSE,
just as we teachers did in the grammar schools, irrespective
as to whether or not it makes sense to them. With those
that attain their various certificates this approach is, of
course, more or less successful. The trouble is that there
are a large number of pupils in our secondary schools who
will not pass these examinations and who prefer to stay
away, or if they attend they are dissatisfied. In my opinion,
it is not difficult to see why they are troublesome.

To give thought to the meaningfulness of lessons to the
children we teach should not, however, be confused with
allowing them to work only when they wish. On the
contrary, once both teacher and pupils know the purposes
of the lesson, the teacher can demand that his pupils work
hard even if they do not like the task. This is an essential
part of learning. Overcoming resistance to work gives a
pupil great satisfaction and the teacher will feel justified in
encouraging his pupils to do so as long as both the teacher
and the taught know that it is worth while.

11
Class management and the emotional development of the child

The interesting and meaningful lesson might be considered the basis for smooth class management, but this by itself will not suffice. There are other and more subtle factors involved, factors that are more closely linked to the feelings and to the way feelings are expressed in large groups.

In contemporary thought there is a tendency to divide cognitive activities, such as learning, from feeling. When we talk about teaching to read, or learning a foreign language or becoming acquainted with historical facts, we hardly ever consider that the teacher and the pupil will also feel about what they are *doing*, irrespective of the feelings they might have for each other. Yet we all have the experience that we learn better if we 'feel' like it, and cannot concentrate if we do not, and that we cannot always account for these feelings.

Emotional aspects are, of course, inherent in every cognitive activity and therefore in every part of the school curriculum. This applies to the learning as well as the teaching. Hence the 'Prospero-teacher' with Ariel's suggestive power is more likely to involve the pupils' feelings than the teacher who regards himself as an instructor. This is, of course, most apparent in those subjects of the curriculum such as art, music or literature, which are connected with art and artists in the widest sense, so that the subject matter itself is inevitably concerned with feelings. Through experiencing feelings through these media, we will find it easier to come to terms with the same feelings in ourselves.

The value of 'oblique' discussions of unacceptable feelings for the pupil–teacher relationship

Let me give an example. Let us consider Othello's intense feelings of jealousy. Feelings of jealousy are, of course, very common, yet most of us do not wish to admit to these feelings. If we do, it is extraordinarily difficult to give these feelings appropriate expression. One feels that one wishes to destroy either the rival or the person one loves or both, and if one does one has the strongest feelings of guilt.

Othello destroys the person he loves and then destroys himself. This enables us to experience the emotions and tortures of jealousy and also the retribution that our conscience demands.

In suggesting the study of *Othello* the teacher gives an unspoken message, which goes somewhat like this: 'I think this is a play worth studying. I approve of the feelings expressed. I approve of feelings of jealousy.' It therefore gives the message that feelings of jealousy are acceptable. It also gives the reader the opportunity for the feelings of catharsis that are mentioned by Aristotle as one of the values of tragedies. The destruction of the hero is a satisfying experience because it is the consequence of his guilt. So the reader has the satisfaction of experiencing the feelings and the punishment by proxy.

It might be said that pupils studying *Othello* have not experienced the jealousy between husband and wife. I think that is immaterial. All children experience jealousy in plenty, right from the beginning when they have to share the attention of their mother with their siblings and their father. In the classroom situation itself the pupils experience the same jealousy in relationship to the teacher. They would like his undivided attention. They do not wish to share him. They want him to like them best.

When these feelings of jealousy become too acute they wish to destroy the teacher, just as Othello destroys Desdemona. So while they are discussing Othello's feelings towards Desdemona they could be said to be discussing their own feelings towards the teacher and their own experiences of jealousy since early childhood. If they act the play themselves, they will of course experience these feelings more vividly. As the teacher approves of Othello's feelings, he indirectly also approves of the children's. He also demonstrates that feelings are different from action. Othello destroys himself by killing Desdemona, not by feeling jealous. In this way the children can express their feelings of jealousy to the teacher in this indirect way, and the teacher can show them ways in which these feelings of jealousy can be expressed safely. So the children no longer need to challenge him directly. This will, of course, help them to come to terms with their feelings of jealousy outside the classroom as well, so that the study of *Othello* does not only assist the teacher's class management, it helps towards the emotional stability of the child in general. Of course, it only helps within limits. Attention-seeking children who constantly disturb the lesson will not suddenly become docile because of the study of *Othello*. But it will help a little, and the emotional appeal will add to the interest of the lesson. The children will of course not be aware of this interaction, nor would it be of much use to them if they were. A teacher is very often aware of the atmosphere of co-operation and enthusiasm in the classroom, but rarely asks what might account for it.

The effect of 'oblique' discussions on class control

Yet in respect to class control, this way of directing unacceptable feelings to the material is, to my mind, of the greatest assistance to the teacher. It is one of the most effective ways in which feelings can be expressed and yet kept safe. This is of the utmost importance if we consider the intensity of the feelings engendered by a large group, and the importance of the teacher in helping the child to come to terms with his ambivalent and conflicting feelings. These two elements are very closely connected. The teacher can only bear the conflicting feelings if they do not do any harm, yet the large group, the class, is a setting in which ambivalent feelings, particularly those of hostility, can be expressed so strongly that hardly anybody could bear them. Anybody who has experienced a class being out of control will know what this means, and most of us have experienced this at one time or another.

Of course, what I am saying is nothing new. It is happening all the time, without teachers realising it. When I was training to be a teacher, I spent a period of three weeks teaching 6-year-olds in one of the slum areas of London. There were forty children in the class. They were not particularly difficult, but I found it very hard to establish control. They kept disappearing to the lavatory across the playground and not coming back, and I only discovered this at the end of the lesson. There was one exception: nothing of this sort happened when I told them a story and combined it with acting or drawing. My supervisors commented on this, but could not find a reason for it. I wonder whether this phenomenon had not been due to the fact that the stories gave the children this opportunity to experience those feelings they could not accept, and helped them to express these feelings through their acting and drawing, not only just to anybody, but to me, the teacher, who was able to notice it and to accept it as good.

Ways of facilitating expression of feelings

Nowadays, in my work as a supervisor of trainees who are taking small groups of emotionally disturbed children with severe reading disability, I encourage this aspect of teaching systematically and the students are often greatly surprised at its effectiveness. Some students find it difficult at first to accept the link between the children's more acceptable behaviour and the kind of activities they introduce, even though the groups are small and they can observe the children's behaviour much more closely than a teacher in a large class is able to do. Most of them, however, begin to see the connection after a while and become very inventive in devising different activities to facilitate the expression of those feelings that, according to their observation, the children need to express.

If teachers in school were more aware of this link between the content of their lesson and the children's behaviour they, too, might give more thought to the emotional aspects of their lesson. A teacher of English confronted with a rebellious class of teenagers, might for instance, choose to read *Julius Caesar* with them rather than *A Midsummer Night's Dream*.

Feelings experienced in repetitive practice of skills

The principles adhering to those parts of the curriculum that lend themselves to expression of feelings such as music, art and literature, can also be applied to the most repetitive activities which seem to have no affinity to feelings at all.

I should like to give as an example our way of practising lists of words with children who are backward in reading. It could be expected that these children would avoid this activity as best they can, but they are usually quite enthusiastic about it. This practice is generally done in the form of a competitive game. The child scores the words correctly read, the teacher the mistakes. The game is not introduced unless the teacher is sure that the child will score far more than he does. There has never been a case where this simple device has been known to fail, as long as the competition is with the teacher and not with another child. Yet it is not a gimmick. The effectiveness of the activity lies in the relationship it creates between the teacher and the child. They are in competition and the child 'beats' the teacher, the adult towards whom he has ambivalent feelings. The teacher accepts the 'beating' without hesitation, even with relish, for the teacher's defeat is linked to the child's success in having mastered what the teacher wanted the child to learn. So it is the teacher's success, too. In this way the child does the necessary practice and has an opportunity to come to terms with ambivalent feelings in a way the teacher can accept.

The teacher's feelings about himself as an authority figure

There is another aspect of the interrelationship between the teacher and his class connected with the teacher's feelings. The tutors supervising my school practice of the 6-year-olds in London also remarked that they thought that, most of the time, I was terrified of the children. This was so, and I was aware that the terror abated in my story lessons, although neither my tutors nor I could account for that. Perhaps I was unconsciously aware of the children's hostile feelings and afraid of their hostility? Perhaps, when these feelings could be expressed in the indirect way through the stories, I felt more secure without knowing it? I think this is highly probable, and to the extent to which this was true, in my case, it may be true in general.

This is perhaps the most intangible part of class management. For the teacher, being human, also has ambivalent feelings towards the pupils in his class and again, being human, he is not aware of all of them. As each human being is unique, it cannot be predicted precisely what these feelings might be.

There are, however, some feelings which are likely to be aroused on account of the situation : these are particularly the teacher's own feelings about authority. We all have very mixed feelings about authority, because we were all, at one time, dependent on those in authority over us. Being in authority is nothing wicked, and it must not be confused with being authoritarian. All parents have authority over their children and so do teachers who are, after all, *in loco parentis*. Basically this means that they are responsible for their children's action and for keeping them out of harm. This, however, implies that children have, at times, to do certain things that they do not like to do. Young children, for instance, have to go to bed to get enough sleep, often when they feel that now is the best time to play. This parental behaviour makes usually no sense to them. Similarly, parents like their teenagers to be home at a certain time in the evening, usually for very good reasons, yet the teenagers regard this parental demand as an interference with their freedom. There are many occasions like these, all of them resulting in feelings of resentment towards the person in authority, who is, at the same time, a person profoundly loved. Again, each of us has to come to terms with his or her ambivalent feelings, and nobody will have solved this dilemma to perfection.

The effect of the teacher's feelings on class control

This has, I think, a profound effect on class management. The teacher, as a person in authority, also makes demands on children that do not make sense to them, although they may be perfectly reasonable. Take, for instance, the question of noise. It is to my mind quite reasonable to keep the noise level within certain limits, at certain times, yet the children do not see the reason for it, at least not always. So the teacher cannot escape their resentment. The teacher's ability to handle this situation will therefore greatly depend on the extent to which he has been able to come to terms with his own ambivalent feelings about authority. It is particularly hard for the young teacher who has hardly outgrown his own adolescence and might feel far more sympathetic towards the rebelling children than towards his colleagues, who share with him the burden of being in the position of authority. Not infrequently the young teacher attempts to be extremely kind and understanding only to find that the children are far more rebellious towards him than they are towards some of his much less sympathetic colleagues. Because he has identified with the pupils and has refused to face his role as the person in authority, the pupils feel insecure and let their feelings be known.

This kind of situation easily sets off a chain reaction. The teacher is angry and disappointed with the children, although he might not permit himself to be aware of this. After all, he wanted to become a teacher because he was fond of children, so he cannot admit that he has hostile feelings. He is also afraid that those in authority over him, e.g. the head, might find out that he cannot keep control. This is particularly true in regard to noise, as a quiet class often symbolises a class under control, sometimes with very little justification. As one becomes more experienced one begins to differentiate between a 'working noise' and a noise that indicates a group of children out of control, but not all experienced teachers would agree with this statement. With so many anxieties besetting the teacher, it is not difficult to see that he will be unable to find a solution to the situation, if the children become troublesome. This was precisely what had happened to me with my group of 6-year-olds. I remember dreading getting up in the morning, because I felt I was not able to meet the challenge of my working day.

What can be done?

Basically, the only remedy in my opinion is to become aware of one's feelings. In a very paradoxical way one's reactions are automatically much more appropriate when one knows what one is feeling than if one rejects having the feeling altogether. If one *feels* angry with another person one need not necessarily *be* angry with him. One might even come to understand that he cannot help being objectionable. However, this is hard to believe without having experienced it. In my case, I continued to have some difficulties for several years, until I began to understand two aspects of my behaviour: first of all, I realised that I reacted in an aggressive way whenever a child became aggressive. It amazed me how quickly the situation improved once I had realised what I was doing. Second, I came to the conclusion that I never expected the children to do what I told them, yet I felt I was unable to give them a 'good' lesson if they could not accept my arrangements for organisation, however trivial these might be. Again, to my greatest amazement they began to follow my directions. Nor did I feel that they resented it. On the contrary, both they and I were much happier.

I do not think that this change was solely the result of my having accepted my position of authority. I think it is much more complicated than that and my understanding of the dynamics in this case is still very limited.

Yet to my mind there are these two main factors that appear to be the key to class management: the 'good' lesson and the understanding of the children's feelings and of one's own. A great deal is being taught about the 'good' lesson. There are plenty of books and courses in methods of teaching in all areas of the curriculum.

However, little has been written about the emotional meaning of the curriculum. I myself have written in greater detail about it elsewhere (Caspari, 1970). Similarly, little attention has been given to the ways of gaining insight into the feelings of other people and of oneself, although interest in these aspects of the interrelationships is becoming more popular. Some of these ways will be explored in the next chapter.

12
Towards increasing insight and understanding

Many examples in this book have illustrated how intricately the process of learning is connected with feelings, feelings about learning, the children's feelings towards the teacher and vice versa. The learning process that was discussed was connected with skills and facts, the learning of reading and writing, the learning of our natural and geographical environment, of the history of nations and so on. In contrast, this chapter focuses primarily on the learning of insight into feelings.

'Learning about feelings': difficulties in communication

Such a discussion is, of course, fraught with difficulties because the 'learning about feelings' requires a different dimension from the more factual learning mentioned above. It is obviously not sufficient to 'think' about feelings, one has to 'feel' them, and how is one going to increase somebody else's capacity to 'feel about feelings'? How is one going to communicate about the process?

I am very much aware of the difficulty of this task, and I beg the reader to be patient if my attempt to discuss this matter does not completely satisfy his curiosity. After all it stands to reason that one cannot feel about feelings by an objective discussion such as this. This difficulty is encountered by all of us in connection with aesthetic experiences. If one has been to a really wonderful concert or to a superb performance of a play, one is always frustrated by one's inability to communicate this experience to anyone else who was not there. Whatever one says, the account seems to fall flat. In other words, one can explain what has happened, but not what it has meant to oneself.

Just as learning in general takes place in various settings, so does learning about feelings. Children do not learn only by systematic instruction in school. They learn constantly by living and a particular child might learn more by picking up and examining a fallen leaf in the autumn or by observing a bird on his way to school than by a carefully planned lesson.

Informal ways of increasing insight and understanding

Similarly, insight and understanding can be increased just as successfully in informal ways as by attending a course. In the school setting, for instance, such learning can occur if a teacher is able to talk about his own difficulties to someone he can trust to remain sympathetic and understanding and not to despise him for having problems.

Young teachers often find a particular member of staff whom they can trust in this way, and receive much help from him. More important still is the sympathetic understanding of the head towards these problems. I know of several infant school heads who are fulfilling this role with great success and carry it out in a number of ways. Some of them arrange to see a young teacher individually and help her while discussing the curriculum and different ways of teaching. Other heads have regular meetings with the whole staff or with the staff of a year group and encourage teachers to discuss their problems. It seems that such arrangements are easier in infant schools than in schools for older children, probably because it is easier to accept that young children behave in undesirable ways. Besides, there are more systematic studies in the development of young children than of any other age range.

Finally, I think that, by and large, more effective training is given to infant school teachers than to teachers of older children, so both the young teacher and his adviser are likely to feel more secure. For it is not only important for the inexperienced teacher to be able to admit that he or she has problems, the experienced teacher needs also to be in touch with the young teacher's difficulties. Young teachers, for instance, are usually very preoccupied with discipline problems. Many experienced teachers, on the other hand, declare that they never have any problems about control. Only the most secure teacher admits to such difficulties, usually in terms of strain. 'One can never let up with these children', Mrs B, a very skilful teacher in an educational priority area school, confessed to me when she retired. One never would have guessed this by watching her interact with her class. She was so relaxed and friendly and the children so spontaneous and natural. She had been a great help to many teachers in the school.

Discussion of practical experience as a basis for training

However, this kind of informal help is rather haphazard, and it is therefore useful to look more closely at some of the more systematised situations that are set up to increase insight and understanding of other people's feelings and of one's own. I shall restrict this discussion to what is available to teachers, and I shall give some examples from my own experience.

All the more formalised schemes of training that I know have some underlying principles in common: the training is based on the trainee's practical experience which he offers for discussion. This may be an account of the behaviour of a difficult child, it may be an account of part of a lesson, or of an interview with parents or with another teacher. Some training schemes also provide some direct experience of interaction. In all schemes this direct experience is the basis of study and is shared between the reporter and somebody else who is able to use this experience to increase insight and understanding. Sometimes this process is used within a recognised training scheme, sometimes it is part of an advisory or consultative service. In order to be effective there needs to be a relationship of trust between the participants and it is part of the skill of the adviser or trainer to bring about this atmosphere of trust.

The Neighbourhood Schools' Service of the Tavistock Clinic

I should like to start with an account of my own work as an educational psychologist. In this role I meet, of course, very frequently the teacher's problems with difficult children, particularly with children who do not make progress in learning and with those that disrupt the learning/teaching process by their difficult behaviour. I think there are great similarities between my work and that of school counsellors, advisers and inspectors.

The special setting for my work as an educational psychologist is that of a clinic under the National Health Service concerned with helping children with emotional problems and their parents. In connection with this work the school of every child patient is contacted with the permission of the parents. In addition, we developed some more intensive direct contact with some schools.

There are two main aspects to this service: it is an attempt to mobilise the resources of the school and the clinic to help those children who are a problem to their teachers, to themselves and generally, though not always, to their parents as well. This aspect of the service is described in some detail elsewhere (Caspari and Osborne, 1967). In this discussion I should like to concentrate on the other main aim: that of helping the teacher and the head to increase their understanding of these children and enable them to use their skills more effectively in their own contact with these difficult children. This is, of course,

116

not a one-way process. I learn as much from the teachers and the head as they learn from me; most importantly, I am kept in constant contact with the reality of schools, with the teachers' trials and tribulations, with their inventions and creative educational thinking, with the joy of discovery and of acquiring skills.

When the head or the teacher is seen, the direct experience of interaction is usually provided by an account of the child's behaviour in class or in the head's study, or an account of the teacher's or head's contact with the parents, or a combination of these. Usually there is also some information about the home and the family that can be gleaned from the school file and the medical file. Neither of these are very easy to get. The teachers' reports are often phrased in general terms: 'Johnny is very disruptive', 'The parents were very unco-operative.' In order to be helpful, it is important for all of us to know what Johnny and his parents actually did and said. The judgment of the reporter is usually quite correct, but only the details will enable us to increase our understanding of Johnny's behaviour and that of his parents.

Nina, an example of school consultation

For instance, one teacher had a problem with a 15-year-old girl who constantly swore in class. The teacher had had her in his class for a year. She was described as tall, neat and clean, not very good at anything in school. She had very bad posture. She was shy and self-conscious in individual contact with the teacher, but she constantly quarrelled with her classmates. The teacher described how he recently had made quite a harmless remark about some painting that Nina had done. He could not quite make out some of the details. Nina immediately construed this remark as a criticism and released a string of 'filthy language'. The teacher did not find it surprising that she had few friends. He said there was only one girl who did not seem to mind the swearing.

The teacher had tried to solve the problem by visiting the family in an attempt to mobilise the parents' help. This attempt had failed. The parents did not see it as a problem that concerned them. If Nina swore at school, it was the school's business to prevent her doing so.

The teacher had talked to Nina about her swearing many times and had felt that, recently, he had been able to gain her confidence. Nina had told him that she had thought he was cross with her. After that he had noticed that she often tried to have physical contact with him, sidling up to him when he was correcting her work, or walking very close to him in the playground.

After listening to this story I felt that the teacher was most perturbed by the attitude of the parents, and we tried to puzzle out what might be the underlying reason for this apparent apathy. Maybe Nina did not swear at home? Maybe both parents swore frequently themselves and saw nothing wrong with it? Did the teacher and I not swear at times? I certainly did, but there were occasions when it seemed appropriate and there were others when it was not.

In this way we were able to discuss what the teacher felt about Nina's swearing. In this discussion I was very much aware of this problem in general. I knew from experience that most teachers felt very strongly about swearing, understandably so, because many children, particularly adolescents, use swearing as a very effective way of hurting the teacher. Why they succeed so easily I have never quite been able to find out, partly because my contact with adolescents in school as a teacher is limited to grammar school girls, and in the days of 11-plus selection, very few adolescents who used swearing in this kind of aggressive way would ever have been able to pass.

The teacher and I then explored the possible reasons for Nina's swearing and came to the conclusion that she probably did it to attract the teacher's attention. We linked this up with her attempt to get physical contact with him, and decided that her behaviour was much more like that of a young child's who wanted to be patted, although at Nina's age there was also an element of sexuality. By this time the teacher recognised this girl as a child who had probably been very deprived of parental affection in her early childhood, although neither of us had any factual evidence of this. One needs to have a great amount of detail to establish the reasons for this kind of deprivation. It can happen in families that are very concerned about their children. It can happen because of a parent's illness, because of a grandparent's death, because of a mother's unrealistic expectation of her baby's behaviour, because of marital difficulties and a host of other reasons. As far as the teacher's handling of Nina was concerned, the underlying reasons did not seem to matter greatly. It became apparent to him that she needed praise above everything else and that she needed individual attention by an adult in an acceptable way. If she felt that remarks by her classmates about herself were critical, she surely thought that she was not much good. We also discussed whether it would be possible to arrange for some individual remedial teaching for her with a remedial teacher who worked in the school.

Whether or not Nina's swearing decreased subsequently I was never able to find out. She was never mentioned again, but in my position one never knows whether this silence is due to the disappearance of the problem, or whether one's discussion was felt so irrelevant that the teacher thought it was useless. Much depends on the severity of the child's disturbance, in this case, whether Nina could be helped within the framework of her school, or whether she needed a different kind of help. So I wait and see. If such a child is mentioned again, it might be appropriate to make a more thorough investigation. At this point we felt it was better to see whether the teacher was able to help.

This kind of discussion can be even more effective if it is done with a group of teachers. It can then reach more people at the same time. It is also frequently easier for a person to examine his own feelings when other people's problems are discussed.

An account such as this illustrates what was said between us, but it cannot tell what the teacher felt about it. Swearing is meaningful to all of us. Our elders have told us not to swear when we were children, yet a man who does not accept swearing in a pub will be despised by his mates. Could such a discussion help one to gain more understanding of one's feelings? Did it help the teacher to gain more understanding of the child? Did it help to make him more understanding of other children who swear? Was he able to deal with swearing children more effectively?

All these questions have to remain unanswered. Yet this dilemma is common to all teaching. Attainment can be measured objectively, and that, as we all know, is only a part of education. Whether or not the children's value system and attitudes have been influenced by our teaching, we can never find out for certain. We think it does, because we know that our own teachers have done so. There is, at present, no possibility of putting our hunch to the test. Similarly, we can never know whether or not our understanding of the children's feelings has been able to help them come to terms with some of their emotional problems. Sometimes there is enough evidence to suggest that this is so. The striking academic improvement of the group of adolescent girls after the discussion on crushes quoted earlier is a case in point. Yet the improvement might have been due simply to the girls growing up, or to any other event outside school and unknown to me.

Training courses in inter-personal relationships

Nevertheless, there is a growing body of opinion that the

understanding of inter-personal relationships is an important part of professional skills for those of us who spend
most of our time in working with people. There are an
ever-growing number of training courses, some of them
part-time evening events, some of them short residential
full-time courses, some of them tailor made for a particular
profession, some of them interdisciplinary, some run by
special institutions, others arranged by LEAs. Some of
these experiences are incorporated in professional conferences, usually in the form of discussion groups which are
run in a way which promotes the deepening of the participants' awareness of his feelings in relationship to a particular topic. This is, of course, very skilful work and a
superficial discussion of the skills involved in leading these
'enabling groups' is likely to lead to misunderstandings.

*A conference of the English New Education Fellowship: an
example*

The 'enabling groups' I attended were mainly part of conferences of the World Education Fellowship, and its
English section, the English New Education Fellowship.
These conferences often include 'creative activities', such
as painting, writing, pottery and movement. Just as I have
argued earlier that subjects like art, painting and music
enable children to come to terms with their unacceptable
feelings and therefore increase their ability to learn more
effectively, the creative work at the conference also
increased the effectiveness of the 'enabling groups'.

A personal example might throw some light on the
process. I was a group leader during a conference on
authority in education, a topic that aroused deep feelings
in all teachers, as it is connected with one's ability to keep
control. I was also a member of a pottery group and decided
to make a clay model of a male figure sitting cross-legged
in great splendour, symbolising authority. As the figure
emerged, I realised that the front of the figure was that of

a man, while the back was very obviously that of a female. It was clear that I had to make a decision. I opted for the female and ended up with a model of a relaxed female figure, legs to one side, hands resting on her knees. At the time, I was not at all concerned about the meaning of the change and it did not seem important to me to become aware of the conflicts with which I was obviously coming to terms while making this model. I think this is important because it is often felt that coming to terms with contradictory feelings must necessarily include intellectual understanding. I should like to suggest that, particularly in expression work, the working through of the conflict can take place without any intellectual understanding at all. The degree to which the individual has been able to come to terms with the conflict will show in the artistic level of the work, i.e. whether it is successful if judged by aesthetic criteria. I was myself very pleased with the female model and when it was exhibited together with the other work accomplished during the conference, it gained considerable approval from other people. Of course, I could not have achieved this success without the help of the instructor who assisted me on the technical level. This was of great importance to me and is, I think, equally important to the children we teach. If a teacher stimulates a child to express his feelings in art, writing, modelling and so on, the child will be disappointed and discouraged if the technical level of his 'creation' is below the standard he expects of himself. This is even more important for an adolescent or an adult whose expectations might be quite high.

In retrospect, I think that the experience of making this model helped me to some degree to come to terms with my concern about being in authority as a group leader and about being a woman. It did not remove that conflict. These kind of experiences very rarely do, but, I think, it did help me in connection with the task of being a group leader at this conference. Whether or not this experience increased my skills in leading the group is difficult to say. Besides, other members of the group had similar experiences and might in similar ways have come to terms with some of their conflicts and become more able to look at this difficult topic in a more detached way. There is, at present, no way of proving this connection, because there are so many different factors involved that it is difficult to isolate any particular variable.

'Blind spots'

In order to obtain greater insight and understanding in a certain area of puzzling complexity, such as the theme of this conference, it is important to become aware of one's 'blind spots'. Naturally, one seldom discovers one's own blind spots by oneself. In an 'enabling group' this is therefore the task of the other group members and particularly that of the leader. It naturally arouses a certain amount of resentment and resistance. Nobody likes the idea of having blind spots. It could therefore be argued that my work as group leader was made easier, because some of the resentment could be expressed via the creative activities. In this way resistance was diminished and the process of increasing insight and understanding could proceed. In this case the creative activities were used in a way similar to the use of the curriculum, described earlier, to obtain class control. The difference between resistant adults and troublesome children is perhaps not as great as one might think. The resentment is expressed in different ways, partly because the setting is different. A resisting adult can leave the group, a troublesome child is obliged to attend classes by law. Maybe some of the trouble with our adolescents in school is partly due to keeping them in a setting inappropriate to their maturity?

Supervisory groups for teachers

There are, of course, other training groups for teachers, particularly those that help them to gain insight and understanding into the children's feelings and into their own when dealing with these children. These groups are perhaps most adequately described as 'supervisory' groups. Like patients and clients discussed in supervision by child psychotherapists or social workers, these groups focus on detailed accounts of the participants' own experience with their clients. Following the model of social work, the discussion is focused particularly on a detailed account of a worker's session with a client. In the teacher's case that may be an account of a lesson or of an encounter with a child or a group of children in a counselling role. This discussion may be based on a written report or it may arise within the framework of a more general enabling group. These courses are usually run in the evenings at weekly intervals. The Tavistock organises one in 'Psychological Aspects of Counselling in Schools and Colleges of Further Education' for those teachers in 'counselling' roles such as heads, deputy heads and heads of departments. It runs another in 'Psychological Aspects in the Treatment of Severe Reading Disability' for teachers working in this field. Similar courses are arranged by some local authorities in teachers' centres and by some universities. A description of the techniques in connection with introducing supervisory techniques into teacher training can be found in two articles published in *Education for Teaching* (Caspari and Eggleston, 1965; Clark, 1967).

The articles describe a project in which school practice in a college of education was arranged so that the teacher-in-training met his tutor once a week to discuss with him the written reports of one of his lessons. This report was discussed with special reference to the interaction between the teacher and his pupils in relationship to the learning, to the subject matter, to the content and to the presentation. The group leader of such supervisory groups needs therefore to know as much of the skills of teaching as of human relationships.

Group relations training

In conclusion, I should like to refer to those training groups that concentrate on the study of human behaviour in groups, based on the theories of Bion (1961). These groups focus on the feelings of the group members. A very lucid short description of these groups can be found in Richardson (1973). Generally these experiences are organised for inter-disciplinary groups of people with managerial responsibilities, such as managers in industry, prison governors, civil servants and members of the helping professions. In education, managers are usually found amongst heads, deputy heads, educational advisers, inspectors and education officers. Yet, as class teachers are generally managers of their class, group relations training is also relevant to them. Richardson has adapted this method especially for teachers (1967).

These are but a few examples of training available in this country for teachers who wish to increase their insight and understanding of feelings in relationships, particularly of those that seem irrational. There are not very many of them, but they are on the increase and their number is likely to grow with increased demand.

13

Outside help for children with problems

Even under the most ideal conditions and in spite of the most skilful teaching there will always be troublesome children who need help outside the school.

The importance of parents

It is not always easy for a teacher to know how to set about getting this help. Moreover, procedures differ. They depend on the particular LEA and the area's provision for children with problems. They also vary according to the ways in which a particular school will deal with such problems. The initial approach of the teacher is most usefully made to the head as he or she, as manager of the school, will have to make the contact with the outside agencies and with the parents. Parents are of the utmost importance in this matter. They will have to agree with any plan for outside help, e.g. placement in a special school. Sometimes their agreement to take an active part in the treatment plan is also essential if the child is referred to a Child Guidance Clinic.

Teachers often forget this aspect of the procedure. They see the child's need for help and understandably they want this help for this child as quickly as possible. They cannot understand that the parents might not be so enthusiastic. For instance, if it is considered that treatment at a Child Guidance Clinic would be most appropriate for the child, it is of no avail if the parents are not prepared to attend the clinic as well. Children are taken to the clinic by their parents. If, as a result of the treatment, changes take place in their child, the parents might not be able to bear it, particularly if the child becomes temporarily more difficult to handle at home. So the treatment will be broken off. In order to prepare parents for these changes and to help them with the management of the child at home, parents, too, will have to attend the clinic more or less regularly, and many parents whose children have severe problems are not prepared to do this, sometimes because their own life is so disorganised that they are unable to keep appointments. Therefore it can easily happen that treatment at a Child Guidance Clinic may be considered desirable, yet this treatment plan has to be abandoned because the parents would not be able to carry it through. It is easy to blame the parents and many teachers do. Yet, like the troublesome child, the parents, too, have problems and need sympathy and understanding.

Alternatively, placement in a special school may appear to be the most appropriate remedy for the child. Again, such placement would be of little use if the parents were not to agree.

In very extreme cases, when the parents' behaviour is detrimental to the child's development, it is, of course, possible to take them to court and to have the child put into the care of the local authority. However, this is a very drastic step that one would like to avoid if at all possible.

The need for investigation

All these considerations indicate the importance of a detailed investigation. Usually there are two ways in which this can be done. The head of the school can refer the child to the school medical officer, or he can bring the child to the attention of the educational psychologist. In the first case the school medical officer will see the child and the parents will be encouraged to attend. This procedure, however, is about to change with the re-organisation of the National Health Service. If the head refers the child to the educational psychologist, the psychologist will decide what to do next. He might start by seeing the child at school and observe him in class or he might see him for a psychological investigation at school, after having obtained permission from the parents. Alternatively, he might know that a social worker is in regular touch with the family and he might approach him first.

Problems of investigations and reasons for delay

Much will depend on the services that are available. In some LEAs the school psychological service is so understaffed that it is unrealistic to hope that the educational psychologist might be involved. Similarly, the ways in which referral to special schools can be arranged varies from one LEA to another. In addition, facilities vary. In some areas there is a great variety of special educational facilities: ESN schools, both residential and day, day and residential schools for maladjusted children, schools for delicate children, remedial classes, adjustment classes, tutorial classes, peripatetic teachers and occasionally classes for school refusers. All recommendations for treatment must ultimately depend on what is available, although in the long term recommendations for an increase in facilities might be very useful. In the same way, I have found that heads vary in their skill of working with the social services and the educational psychologist. Some work very closely with the social workers in their district, so that the child can be helped solely through a social worker's regular visits to a family. Sometimes this is the only help the parents can accept.

These investigations often take a considerable time. I expect placement in a school for maladjusted children to take about six to nine months from the time that the head and the teacher have discussed the problem with me at school. The head and I then explore how best to approach the parents. This might necessitate a consultation with some social workers. Alternatively, the head might invite the parents to the school. If the parents consent that the problems of the child might be investigated at the clinic, such an investigation may take several weeks. If the clinic team recommends placement at a special school and the parents agree, a place has to be found, and that might take several months, as there are likely to be long waiting lists.

Other difficulties might hold up treatment. George and Charles, for instance, were 9-year-old twins referred to the clinic for difficult behaviour and inability to learn. There was no father, and mother was very willing to come to the clinic to discuss how to help the twins. She made it very clear that she herself could not attend the clinic because she had to earn a living and look after the house, and the clinic was too difficult to reach from her home. She was quite amenable to the twins having help, but she was unable to bring them. It was decided that educational therapy would be the most adequate mode of treatment for the twins, but it was difficult to lay on transport from the school. The school could only arrange transport for them if the twins could be brought at the same time. So they had to be seen at the same time by two different educational therapists. It took almost six months to arrange this.

So the teacher has to expect that this process will take some time and that the problem child will not receive help immediately. Moreover, if he is thinking of placement, he needs to know that it will be very difficult to place a child in a special school once he has reached the age of 14. Few schools take children of this age. They feel they would need more than two years to be effective.

The need for early referral

For all these reasons it is, I think, preferable for a child to be referred as early as possible, even if the teacher might feel that he will grow out of his difficulty. He might well do so, yet it is useful to start the investigation early even if no treatment is carried out. If the school knows more about the nature of the problem and if the social services are alerted, help can be arranged much more quickly, should it be needed.

The resistance to referral is often connected with the teacher's insecurity. He or she feels that the child's problems are caused by his or her lack of skill in keeping discipline. It is easy to understand why teachers feel as they do. I hope that when the difficulty of class control is more generally appreciated both by teachers and parents, teachers will feel less hesitant to refer problem children earlier, and that, in turn, will make it easier to find adequate help for these children. Referrals are also delayed because of the scarcity of educational psychologists and social workers.

Outside help is therefore not always available in the way described in this chapter, and this discussion has not covered all the various possibilities. Yet, if the services are not available, I should like to encourage teachers to persevere and to make their objections heard. Changes will only come about if there is sufficient pressure. If the teachers just accept adverse circumstances, nobody will know that problems exist. Complaints will, of course, not bring about immediate change, but continuous pressure usually works in the end.

14
Conclusion: the tribulations of teaching and its opportunities

One thing is certain—troublesome children will always be in our classes. This has been so ever since schools were established. The degree of troublesome behaviour might, of course, vary from generation to generation, from school to school, from district to district, from one particular teacher to another. The extent of behaviour disorders within the population at any place or time will, of course, influence the severity of the problem. Yet the teacher himself might find the remedy for these problems by experimenting with new ways of teaching or new ways of organisation and, above all, by taking great trouble about the content and presentation of his lessons.

The present situation

This is, of course, easier in primary schools. We know more about young children and what is interesting to them and important to learn. Society is very unclear about the appropriateness of the curriculum for the young adolescent of our secondary schools. A great deal of thought and experimentation is needed in this area. The present crisis, the increase of truancy and violence in this age-range, may hopefully necessitate fundamental changes in the very near future, to the benefit of generations to come.

Class control is therefore extremely difficult to maintain in our secondary schools at present. To some degree this distorts the fundamental problem. For teachers ought to expect to have troublesome children in any class, just as parents expect their children to be disobedient from time to time. If a child does not try out to what limits he can go, he has not experienced that his parents will keep him from harm and that they make certain demands on him. If the young person misses out on this experience, his development will be impeded. Most parents worry almost as much if their child is too good as if he is too naughty, and they take it as part of their role as parents to deal with disobedience when it occurs. Of course, it is a bother, and no parent deals with this situation successfully all the time, but I think that to some degree the parents accept this bother more easily than do the teachers.

There are many reasons for this, of course, as discussed earlier, particularly in consideration of the parental expectation of the teacher's perfect handling of his pupils.

A change of attitude

As professionals, however, I just wonder whether the teachers themselves could not begin to develop a different attitude in this respect.

If we accept that life is beset by conflicts most of the time, and that a happy and effective person is one who is able to come to terms with these conflicts, is there not great value in giving the child an opportunity to experience some of these conflicts in school and to come to terms with them? The teacher who is able to deal successfully with the rebellious child in his class has not only helped that particular child to come to terms with ambivalent feelings, he has helped all the other members of the class who shared the rebel's feelings but did not dare to express them. If the rebel had not been troublesome, the children would have been denied the experience, and the educational value of school would have been diminished.

The trouble is that, like the parents, the teacher does not

succeed all the time and that the expression of hostility or of any other feeling might be so extreme that the teacher's skills are unable to deal with the situation.

The teacher's unique opportunity of helping troublesome children

Yet the teacher has this unique opportunity of diverting the children's feelings into learning activities, an opportunity not equalled in any other situation. If these opportunities were enhanced by the teacher's understanding, the contribution of education towards the emotional development of children would increase tremendously, even to the extent that many children with severe behaviour problems might actually be helped in the class.

Many teachers in classes in various parts of the country are doing just that at the present moment. Their work is often little known and they are often reticent about speaking about it, mainly because they cannot explain what they are doing. To some degree they know that there is a link between their handling of the children and the improvement of the children's behaviour. But they cannot be certain.

Advantages and disadvantages of the lack of a formula

It would be much more comforting if there were a scientific formula for keeping class control, for finding precise patterns of behaviour to deal with a particular troublesome child, for evaluating the effect that a particular learning activity might have on the behaviour of the children we teach.

Yet this lack of certainty also adds to the excitement of teaching. It makes teaching an adventure, an art and a very personal experience, an experience of growth for the teacher as well as for his pupils.

Each teacher has to find for himself that framework

within which he and the children in his class can develop in safety, within which they can increase their knowledge and skills and within which they can experience the conflicts of living and come to terms with them. This framework is necessarily a very personal one. Each teacher will have to find the framework that is right for himself, and he will have to modify it according to the children he teaches. He will be more successful with some classes and less with others. He will be happier in one particular school and less confident in another. He might prefer a special age group.

Some readers will already have found the framework that is right for them, some others might still be seeking to find it. There are many difficulties and there are no strict guidelines to follow, yet most of us succeed in the end, helped by the knowledge of all the opportunities for development and growth, for adventure and satisfaction that the school day can offer, and assisted, above all, by our genuine concern for the children, especially for those that are troublesome.

Suggestions for further reading

In selecting books for further study I have concentrated on a few key publications. To guide the reader these are organised under a number of self-explanatory headings, which follow the structure of this book. Under each heading the books are arranged in alphabetical order.

I A psychodynamic view of child development

BOWLBY, J. (1958), 'Psycho-analysis and child care', in J. D. Sutherland, ed., *Psychoanalysis and contemporary thought*, London, Hogarth Press; New York, Grove Press, pp. 33-57.

FREUD, S. (1909), 'Analysis of a phobia in a five-year-old boy', in Standard edition, vol, X, London, Hogarth Press, 1955, pp. 15-49.

FREUD, S. (1926), 'Inhibitions, symptoms and anxiety', in Standard edition, vol. XX, London, Hogarth Press, 1961, pp. 77-172.

KLEIN, D. C. K. (1962), 'Problems in adjustment to school', in H. C. Stuart and D. G. Prugh, eds, *The Healthy Child*, Cambridge, Mass., Harvard University Press.

ROBERTSON, J., ed. (1962), *Hospitals and Children: A Parent's-eye view*, London, Gollancz; New York, International Universities Press, 1964.

II Group dynamics and its relevance to education

BION, W. R. (1961), *Experiences in Groups, and Other Papers*, London, Tavistock Publications.

FREUD, S. (1921), 'Group psychology and the analysis of the ego', in Standard edition, vol. XVIII, London, Hogarth Press, 1955, pp. 69-143.

HERBERT, E. L. (1961), 'The use of group techniques in the training of teachers', *Human Relations*, 14, pp. 251-63.

MORRIS, B. S. (1965), 'How does a group learn to work together?', in W. R. Niblett, ed., *How and Why do we Learn?*, London, Faber, pp. 92-119.

RICHARDSON, E. (1967), *The Environment of Learning*, London, Nelson.

RICHARDSON, J. E. (1951), 'An experiment in group methods of teaching English composition', in *Studies in the Social Psychology of Adolescence*, London, Routledge & Kegan Paul.

TURQUET, P. M. (1973), *Threats to Identity in the Large Group: A Study in the Phenomenology of the Individual's Experiences of Changing Membership Status in a Large Group*, London, Tavistock Institute of Human Relations, Doc. no. CASR 904.

III Difficult children

Under this heading the books are divided into various subgroups. There is, of course, a certain amount of overlap.

1 General (including children with behaviour problems)

CHAZAN, M. *et al.* (1974), *The Practice of Educational Psychology*, London, Longman.

RUTTER, M. *et al.*, eds (1970), *Education, Health and Behaviour*, London, Longman.

STOTT, D. H. (1966), *Studies of Troublesome Children*, London, Tavistock Publications.

WILLIAMS, P., ed. (1974), *Behaviour Problems in School: A*

Sourcebook of Readings, University of London Press.

2   Children with learning difficulties

FRANKLIN, A. W. and NAIDOO, S., eds (1970), *Assessment and Teaching of Dyslexic children,* London, Invalid Children's Aid Association.

MORRIS, J. M. (1966), *Standards and Progress in Reading,* Slough, Bucks, National Foundation for Educational Research.

PETERS, M. L. (1970), *Success in Spelling: A Study of the Factors Affecting Improvement in Spelling in Junior Schools,* Cambridge, Institute of Education.

RAVENETTE, A. T. (1968), *Dimensions of Reading Difficulties,* Oxford, Pergamon Press.

REED, M. (1970), 'Deaf and partially hearing children', in P. Mittler, ed., *The Psychological Assessment of Mental and Physical Handicaps,* London, Methuen, pp. 403-41.

REID, J. F. (1972), *Reading: Problems and Practices,* London, Ward Lock Educational.

TANSLEY, A. E. and GULLIFORD, R. (1960), *The Education of Slow Learning Children,* London, Routledge & Kegan Paul.

VERNON, P. E. (1969), *Intelligence and Cultural Environment,* London, Methuen.

3   School refusal

BOWLBY, J. (1973), 'Anxious attachment and the "phobias" of childhood', in *Attachment and Loss, vol. 2: Separation: Anxiety and Anger,* London, Hogarth Press, pp. 258-91.

CLYNE, M. B. (1966), *Absent: School Refusal as an Expression of Disturbed Family Relationships,* London, Tavistock Publications.

EISENBERG, L. (1958), 'School phobia: a study in the communication of anxiety', *American Journal of Psychiatry,* 114, pp. 712-18.

KAHN, J. H. and NURSTEN, J. P. (1964), *Unwillingly to School: The Place of the Child Guidance Clinic in the Treatment of School Phobia,* Oxford, Pergamon Press.

TURNER, B., ed. (1974), *Truancy*, London, Ward Lock Educational.

TYERMAN, M. J. (1968), *Truancy*, University of London Press.

4 Delinquency

ANDRY, R. C. (1960), *Delinquency and Parental Pathology*, London, Methuen.

BOWLBY, J. (1946), *Forty-four Juvenile Thieves: Their Characters and Home Life*, London, Ballière, Tindall & Cox.

BOWLBY, J. (1952), *Maternal Care and Mental Health*, 2nd edition, Geneva, World Health Organisation.

DOUGLAS, J. W. B. *et al.* (1968), *All our Future: A Longitudinal Study of Secondary Education*, London, Peter Davies.

HARGREAVES, D. H. (1967), *Social Relations in a Secondary School*, London, Routledge & Kegan Paul.

PHILLIPSON, C. M. (1971), 'Juvenile delinquency and the school', in W. G. Carson, and P. Wiley, eds, *Crime and Delinquency in Britain*, London, Martin Robertson, pp. 236-58.

STOTT, D. H. (1960), *A Delinquency Prediction Instrument*, University of London Press.

TRASLER, G. (1962), *The Explanation of Criminality*, London, Routledge & Kegan Paul.

WEST, D. J. (1967), *The Young Offender*, Harmondsworth, Penguin Books.

WEST, D. J. and FARRINGTON, D. P. (1973), *Who Becomes Delinquent?*, Second report of the Cambridge Study in Delinquent Development, London, Heinemann.

IV   The difficult child and the teacher

1   The teacher's role in the school

CASPARI, I. E. (1965), *Roles and Responsibilities of Head Teacher and Teaching Staff in Primary Schools*, London, Tavistock Clinic.

DOUGLAS, J. W. B. (1964), *The Home and the Schools*, London, MacGibbon & Kee.

DEPARTMENT OF EDUCATION AND SCIENCE (1967), *Children and Their Primary Schools: A Report of the Central Advisory Council for Education (England)*, (Chairman: Lady Plowden), vol. I, London, HMSO.

EGGLESTON, J., ed. (1974), *Contemporary Research in the Sociology of Education*, London, Methuen.

HOYLE, E. (1969), *The Role of the Teacher*, London, Routledge & Kegan Paul; New York, Humanities Press.

RICHARDSON, E. (1973), *The Teacher, the School and the Task of Management*, London, Heinemann Educational.

WILSON, R. (1962), 'The teacher's role: a sociological analysis', *British Journal of Sociology*, 13, pp. 15-32.

2 Towards increasing insight and understanding: approaches to training

BALINT, M. (1964), *The Doctor, his Patient and Illness*, 2nd edition, London, Pitman Medical.

CASPARI, I. E. and EGGLESTON, S. J. (1965), 'A new approach to supervision of teaching practice', *Education for Teaching*, no. 68, pp. 42-52.

CLARK, J. M. (1967), 'Supervision of teaching practice', *Education for Teaching*, no. 74, pp. 44-50.

IRVINE, E. E. (1959), 'The use of small group discussions in the teaching of human relations and mental health', *British Journal of Psychiatric Social Work*, 5, pp. 26-30.

RICE, A. K. (1965), *Learning for Leadership: Interpersonal and Group Relations*, London, Tavistock Publications.

RICHARDSON, E. (1967), *Group Study for Teachers*, London, Routledge & Kegan Paul.

TIBBLE, J. W. (1959), 'Problems in the training of teachers and social workers', *Sociological Review Monograph*, no. 2, pp. 47-57.

3 The teacher's contribution towards emotional stability of children

CASPARI, I. E. (1970), 'The curriculum: emotional stability. The contribution of the curriculum towards the emotional stability of the child', reprinted from Association of Headmistresses, *Conference Speeches*, Queen Elizabeth Hall, London, June 1970. London, Association of Headmistresses.

CASPARI, I. E. and OSBORNE, E. (1967), 'The Neighbourhood Schools' Service of the Tavistock Clinic', in Schools Council, *Counselling in Schools*, Schools Council Working Paper, no. 15, London, HMSO.

HOURD, M. L. (1972), *Relationship in Learning*, London, Heinemann.

MORRIS, B. S. (1972), *Objectives and Perspectives in Education*, London, Routledge & Kegan Paul.

WINNICOTT, D. W. (1964), *The Child, the Family and the Outside World*, Harmondsworth, Penguin Books.

WINNICOTT, D. W. (1971), *Playing and Reality*, London, Tavistock Publications.

References

BION, W. R. (1961), *Experiences in Groups, and Other Papers*. London, Tavistock Publications.

BLEULER, E. (1910), 'Vortrag über Ambivalenz', *Zentralblatt für Psychoanalyse*, 1, p. 266.

BOWLBY, J. (1946), *Forty-four Juvenile Thieves: Their Characters and Home Life*, London, Bailliére, Tindall & Cox.

BOWLBY, J. (1958), 'Psycho-analysis and child care', in J. D. Sutherland ed., *Psychoanalysis and Contemporary Thought*, London, Hogarth Press; New York, Grove Press, pp. 33-57.

BOWLBY, J. (1973), 'Attachment and Loss', vol. II, *Separation: Anxiety and Anger*, London, Hogarth Press; Institute of Psychoanalysis.

BRYAN, W. L. and HARTER, N. (1899), 'Studies on the telegraphic language: the acquisition of the hierarchy of habits', *Psychological Review*, 6, pp. 345-75.

CASPARI, I. E. (1965), *Roles and Responsibilities of Head Teacher and Teaching Staff in Primary Schools*, London, Tavistock Clinic.

CASPARI, I. E. (1970), 'The curriculum: emotional stability. The contribution of the curriculum towards the emotional stability of the child', reprinted from Association of Headmistresses, *Conference Speeches*, Queen Elizabeth Hall, London, June 1970. London, Association of Headmistresses.

REFERENCES

CASPARI, I. E. and EGGLESTON, S. J. (1965), 'A new approach to supervision of teaching practice', *Education for Teaching*, no. 68, pp. 42-52.

CASPARI, I. E. and OSBORNE, E. (1967), 'The Neighbourhood Schools' Service of the Tavistock Clinic', in Schools Council, *Counselling in Schools*, Schools Council Working Paper no. 15, London, HMSO.

CLARK, J. M. (1967), 'Supervision of teaching practice', *Education for Teaching*, no. 74, pp. 44-50.

DEPARTMENT OF EDUCATION AND SCIENCE (1967), *Children and Their Primary Schools: A Report of the Central Advisory Council for Education (England)* (Chairman: Lady Plowden) vol. I, London, HMSO.

DOUGLAS, J. W. B. (1964), *The Home and the School*, London, MacGibbon & Kee.

DOWNING, J. (1964), *The I.T.A. Reading Experiment*, London, Evans, for University of London Institute of Education. (Also published as *The Initial Teaching Alphabet Reading Experiment*, Glenview, Ill., Scott, 1965.)

DOWNING, J. (1967), *Evaluating the Initial Teaching Alphabet*, London, Cassell.

FREUD, S. (1909), 'Analysis of a phobia in a five-year-old boy', in Standard edition, vol. X, London, Hogarth Press, 1955, pp. 15-49.

FREUD, S. (1921), 'Group psychology and the analysis of the ego', in Standard edition, vol. XVIII, London, Hogarth Press, 1955, pp. 69-143.

FREUD, S. (1926), 'Inhibitions, symptoms and anxiety', in Standard edition, vol. XX, London, Hogarth Press, 1961, pp. 77-172.

GATES, A. I. (1950), *The Improvement of Reading*, 3rd ed., New York, Macmillan.

HERBERT, E. L. (1961), 'The use of group techniques in the training of teachers', *Human Relations*, 14, pp. 251-63.

HOURD, M. L. (1972), *Relationship in Learning*, London, Heinemann.

HOYLE, E. (1969), *The Role of the Teacher*, London, Routledge & Kegan Paul; New York, Humanities Press.

KAHN, J. H. and NURSTEN, J. P. (1964), *Unwillingly to School: The Place of the Child Guidance Clinic in the Treatment of School Phobia*, Oxford, Pergamon Press.

KLEIN, D. C. K. (1962), 'Problems in adjustment to school', in H. C. Stuart and D. G. Prugh, eds, *The Healthy Child*, Cambridge, Mass., Harvard University Press.

MACKAY, D. *et al.* (1970), *Breakthrough to Literacy: Teacher's Manual. The Theory and Practice of Teaching Initial Reading and Writing*, London, Longman, for the Schools Council.

MONROE, M. (1932), *Children who Cannot Read*, Chicago, Ill., University of Chicago Press.

MORRIS, B. S. (1965), 'How does a group learn to work together?', in W. R. Niblett, ed., *How and Why do We Learn?*, London, Faber, pp. 92-119.

MORRIS, B. S. (1972), *Objectives and Perspectives in Education*, London, Routledge & Kegan Paul.

MORRIS, J. M. (1966), *Standards and Progress in Reading*, Slough, Bucks, National Foundation for Educational Research.

MOXON, C. A. V. (1962), *A Remedial Reading Method*, London, Methuen.

PETERS, M. L. (1970), *Success in Spelling: A Study of the Factors affecting Improvement in Spelling in Junior Schools*, Cambridge, Institute of Education.

PRINGLE, M. L. Kellmer (1974), *The Needs of Children*, London, Hutchinson.

RAVENETTE, A. T. (1968), *Dimensions of Reading Difficulties*, Oxford, Pergamon Press.

REED, M. (1970), 'Deaf and partially hearing children', in P. Mittler ed., *The Psychological Assessment of Mental and Physical Handicaps*, London, Methuen, pp. 403-41.

RICHARDSON, E. (1967), *The Environment of Learning*, London, Nelson.

RICHARDSON, E. (1973), *The Teacher, the School, and the Task of Management*, London, Heinemann Educational.

REFERENCES

RICHARDSON, J. E. (1951), 'An experiment in group methods of teaching English composition', in *Studies in the Social Psychology of Adolescence*, London, Routledge & Kegan Paul.

ROBERTSON, J. ed. (1962), *Hospitals and Children: a Parent's-eye View*, London, Gollancz; New York, International Universities Press, 1963.

RUTTER, M. *et al.* eds (1970), *Education, Health and Behaviour*, London, Longman.

STOTT, D. H. (1962), *Programmed Reading Kit*, Glasgow, Holmes and McDougall.

TIBBLE, J. W. (1959), 'Problems in the training of teachers and social workers', *Sociological Review Monograph*, no. 2, pp. 47-57.

TURQUET, P. M. (1973), *Threats to Identity in the Large Group: A Study in the Phenomenology of the Individual's Experiences of Changing Membership Status in a Large Group*, London, Tavistock Institute of Human Relations, Doc. no. CASR 904.

VERNON, P. E. (1969), *Intelligence and Cultural Environment*, London, Methuen.

WILSON, B. R. (1962), 'The teacher's role: a sociological analysis', *British Journal of Sociology*, 13, pp. 15-32.